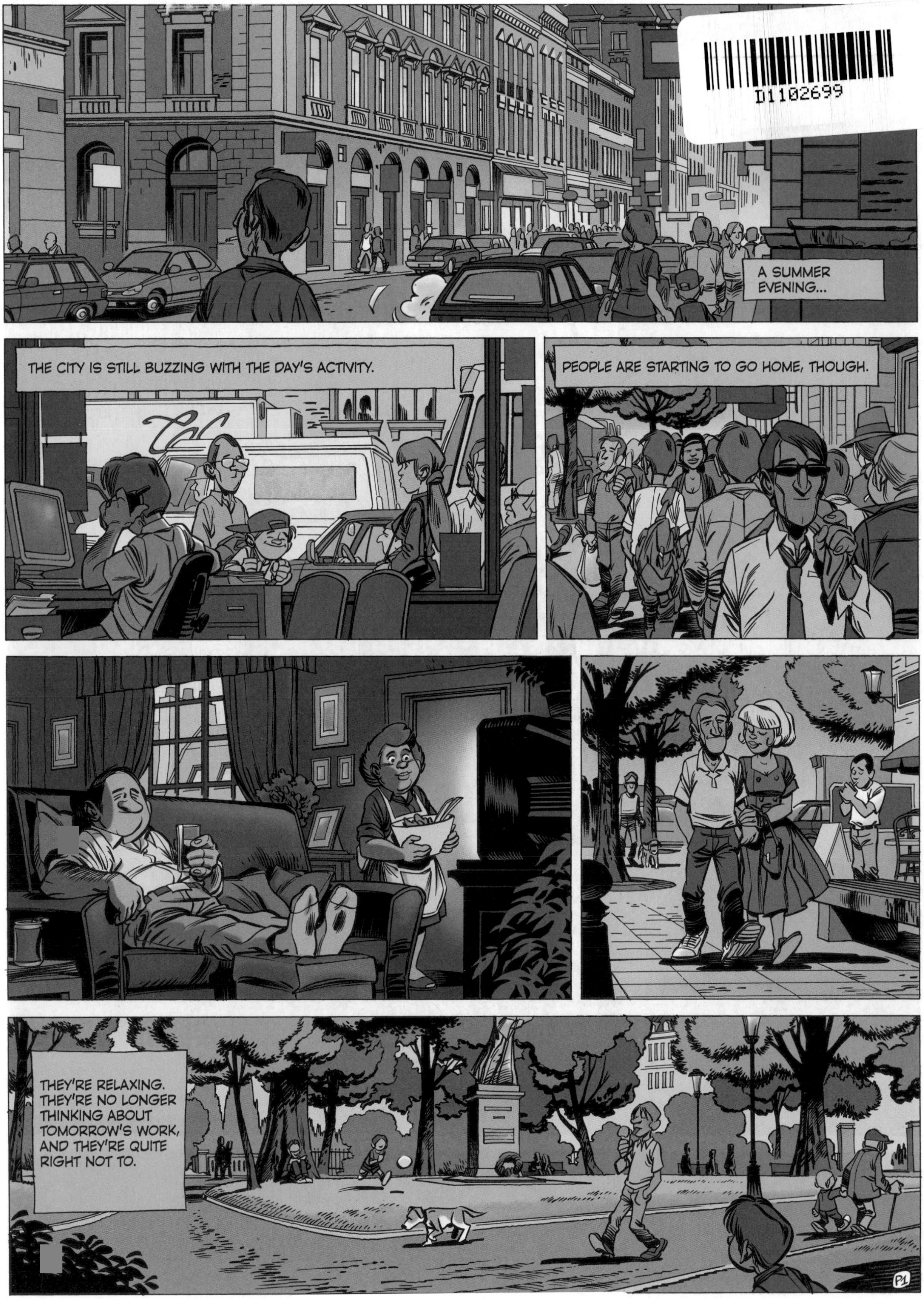

A SUMMER EVENING...
THE CITY IS STILL BUZZING WITH THE DAY'S ACTIVITY.
PEOPLE ARE STARTING TO GO HOME, THOUGH.
THEY'RE RELAXING. THEY'RE NO LONGER THINKING ABOUT TOMORROW'S WORK, AND THEY'RE QUITE RIGHT NOT TO.
P1

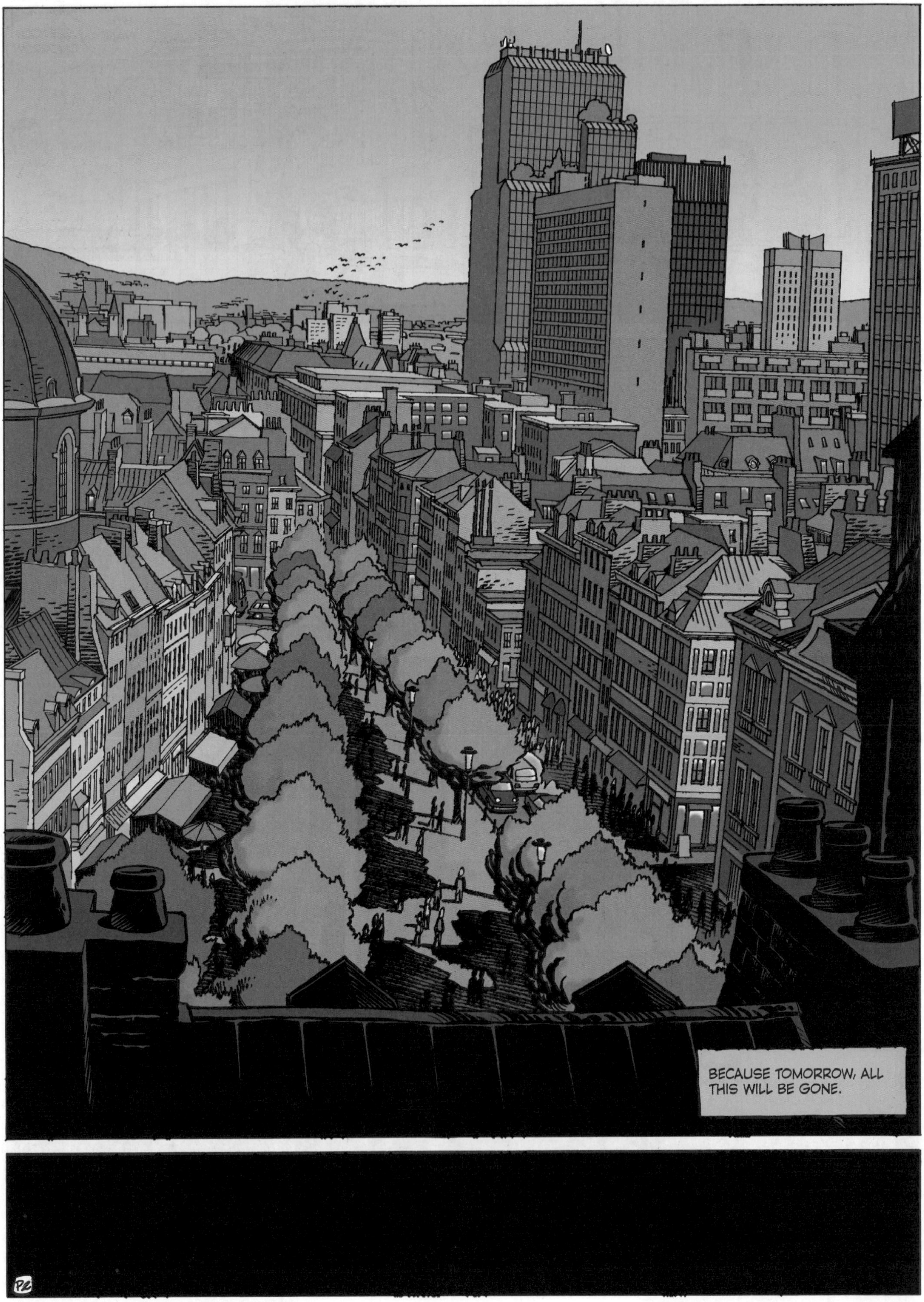
BECAUSE TOMORROW, ALL THIS WILL BE GONE.

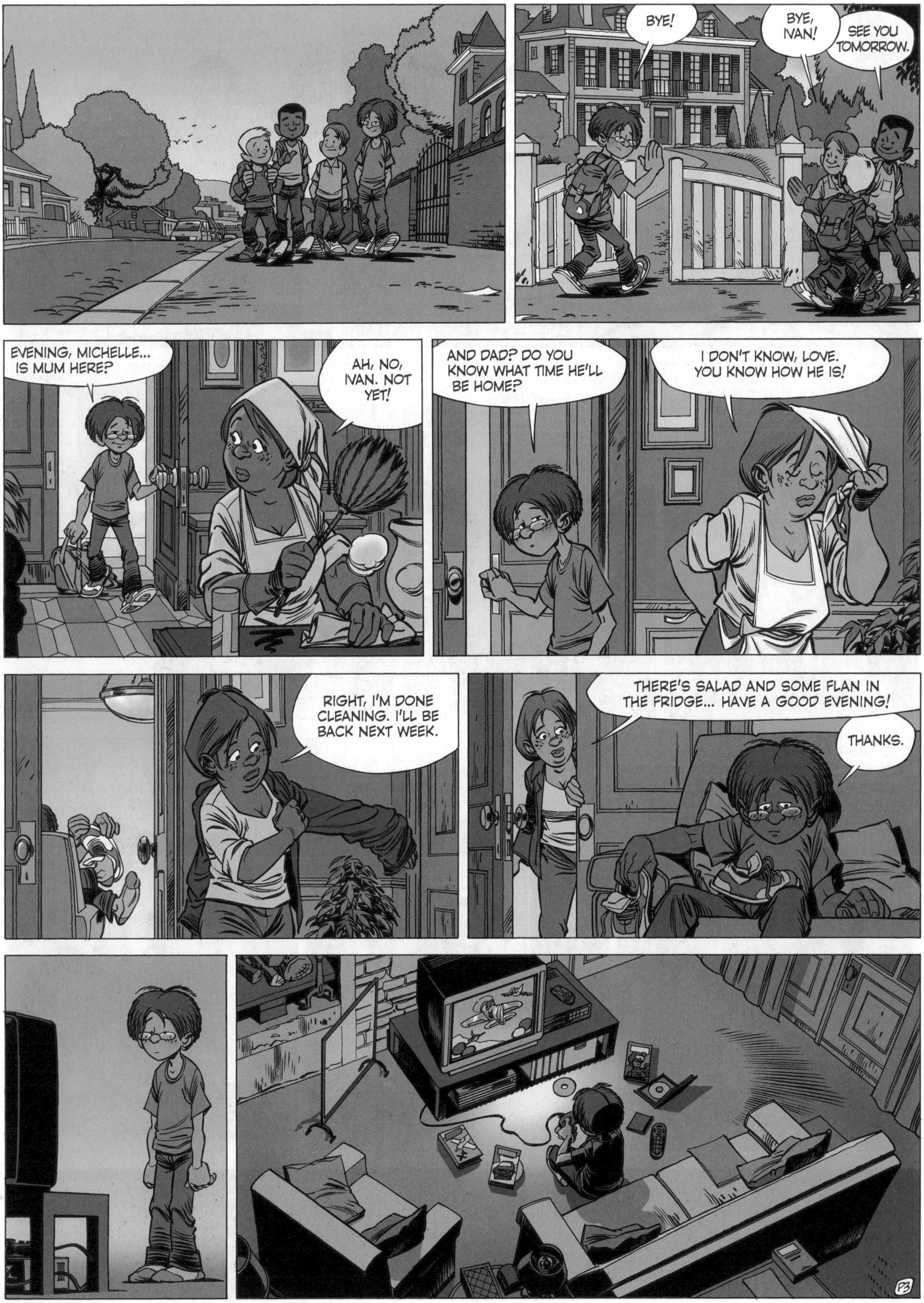

BYE!
BYE, IVAN!
SEE YOU TOMORROW.
EVENING, MICHELLE... IS MUM HERE?
AH, NO, IVAN. NOT YET!
AND DAD? DO YOU KNOW WHAT TIME HE'LL BE HOME?
I DON'T KNOW, LOVE. YOU KNOW HOW HE IS!
RIGHT, I'M DONE CLEANING. I'LL BE BACK NEXT WEEK.
THERE'S SALAD AND SOME FLAN IN THE FRIDGE... HAVE A GOOD EVENING!
THANKS.

HEY, LEILA! WHAT ARE YOU MAKING THIS TIME?

JUST TINKERING.

DON'T YOU THINK IT'D WORK BETTER IF YOU BROUGHT THE WHEEL CLOSER?

DAD...

LOOK, HERE'S YOUR PROBLEM, RIGHT HERE.

DAD, IT'S MY GIZMO! LEAVE ME ALONE, WILL YOU?!

RHAAA! LOOK AT THAT! EVERY TIME!

YEAH, WELL, DON'T COME COMPLAINING IF YOUR THINGY DOESN'T WORK!

ALWAYS FIGHTING, THOSE TWO!

YOU'RE THE ONE WHO BROKE IT!

YEAH, YEAH!

AND THE HEAT ISN'T HELPING.

IT'S TRUE; THE SKY LOOKS WEIRD TONIGHT.

AND LOOK AT THE BIRDS. I'VE NEVER SEEN THEM SO NERVOUS.

IT'S AS IF SOMETHING HAD THEM SCARED.

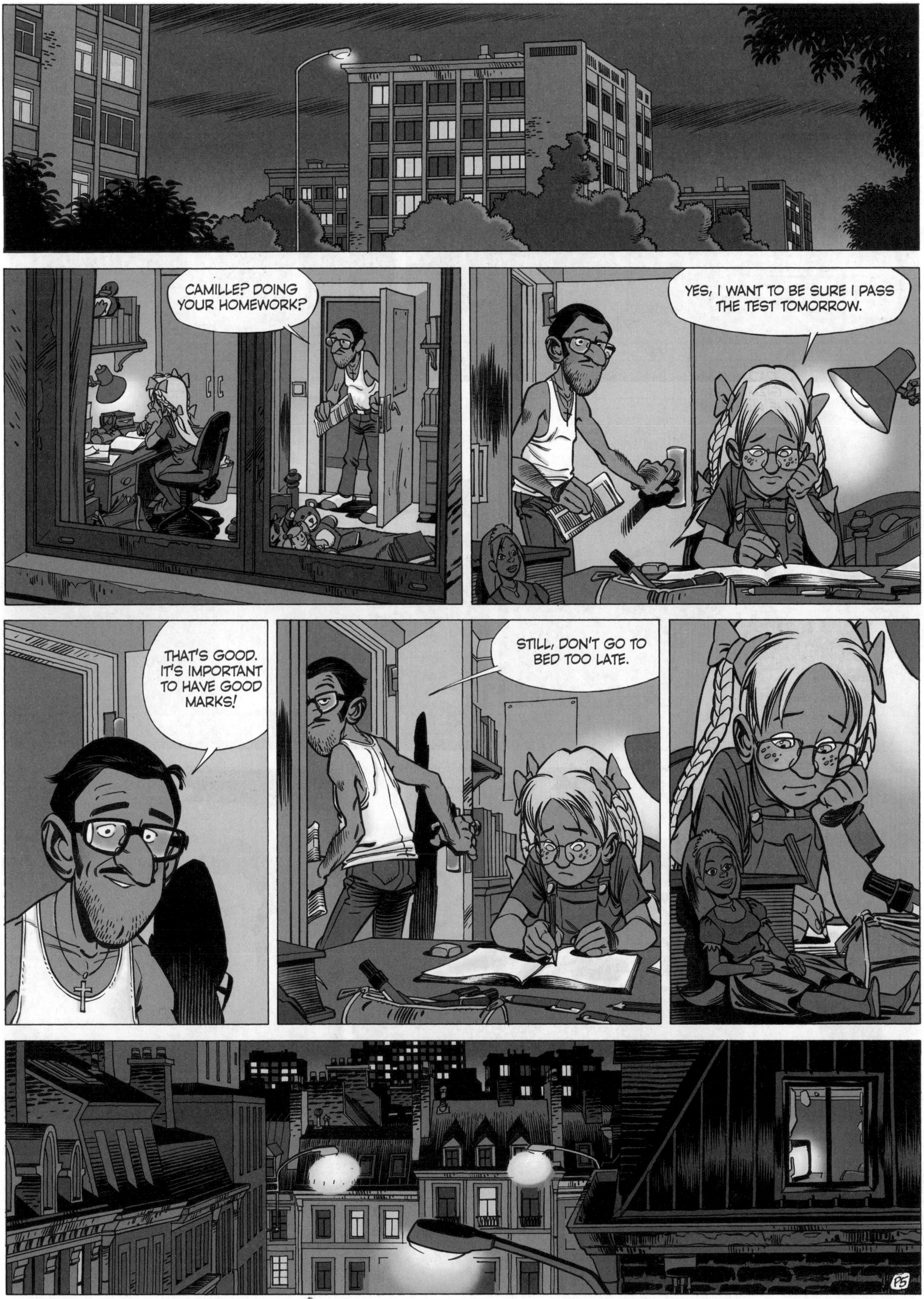
CAMILLE? DOING YOUR HOMEWORK?
YES, I WANT TO BE SURE I PASS THE TEST TOMORROW.
THAT'S GOOD. IT'S IMPORTANT TO HAVE GOOD MARKS!
STILL, DON'T GO TO BED TOO LATE.
P5

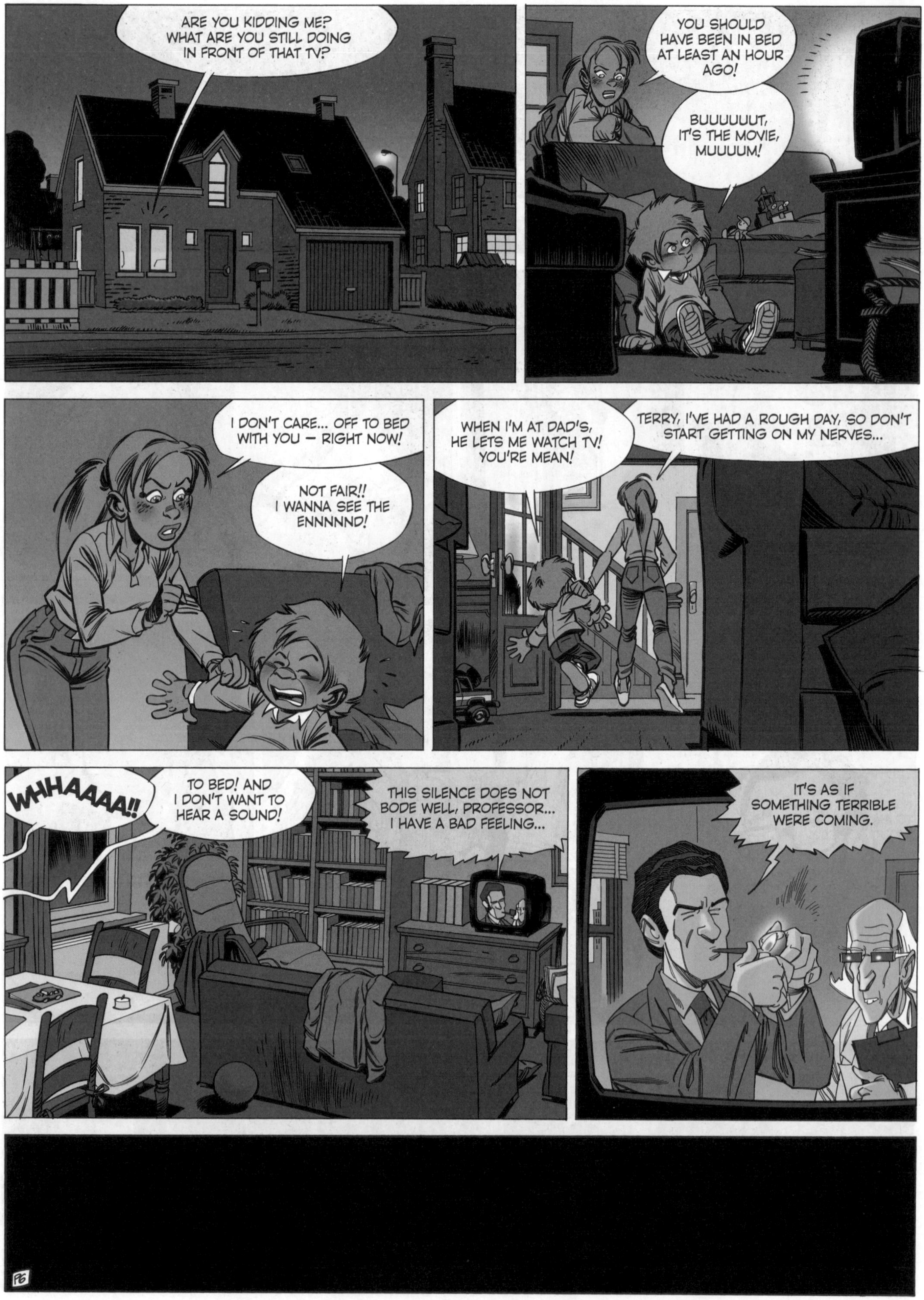
ARE YOU KIDDING ME? WHAT ARE YOU STILL DOING IN FRONT OF THAT TV?
YOU SHOULD HAVE BEEN IN BED AT LEAST AN HOUR AGO!
BUUUUUUT, IT'S THE MOVIE, MUUUUM!
I DON'T CARE... OFF TO BED WITH YOU — RIGHT NOW!
NOT FAIR!! I WANNA SEE THE ENNNNND!
WHEN I'M AT DAD'S, HE LETS ME WATCH TV! YOU'RE MEAN!
TERRY, I'VE HAD A ROUGH DAY, SO DON'T START GETTING ON MY NERVES...
WHHAAAAA!!
TO BED! AND I DON'T WANT TO HEAR A SOUND!
THIS SILENCE DOES NOT BODE WELL, PROFESSOR... I HAVE A BAD FEELING...
IT'S AS IF SOMETHING TERRIBLE WERE COMING.
P6

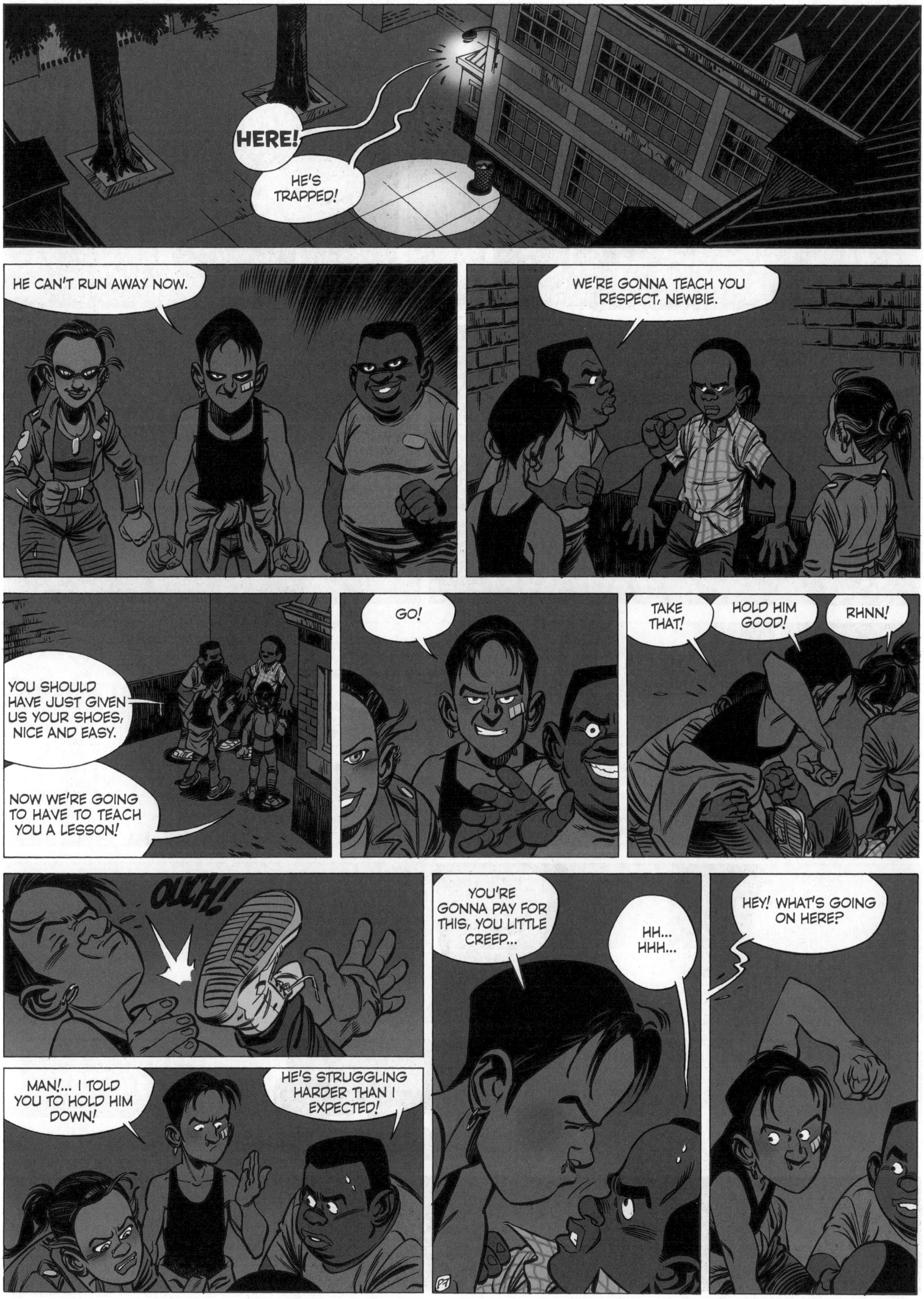
HERE!
HE'S TRAPPED!
HE CAN'T RUN AWAY NOW.
WE'RE GONNA TEACH YOU RESPECT, NEWBIE.
YOU SHOULD HAVE JUST GIVEN US YOUR SHOES, NICE AND EASY.
NOW WE'RE GOING TO HAVE TO TEACH YOU A LESSON!
GO!
TAKE THAT!
HOLD HIM GOOD!
RHNN!
OUCH!
MAN!... I TOLD YOU TO HOLD HIM DOWN!
HE'S STRUGGLING HARDER THAN I EXPECTED!
YOU'RE GONNA PAY FOR THIS, YOU LITTLE CREEP...
HH... HHH...
HEY! WHAT'S GOING ON HERE?

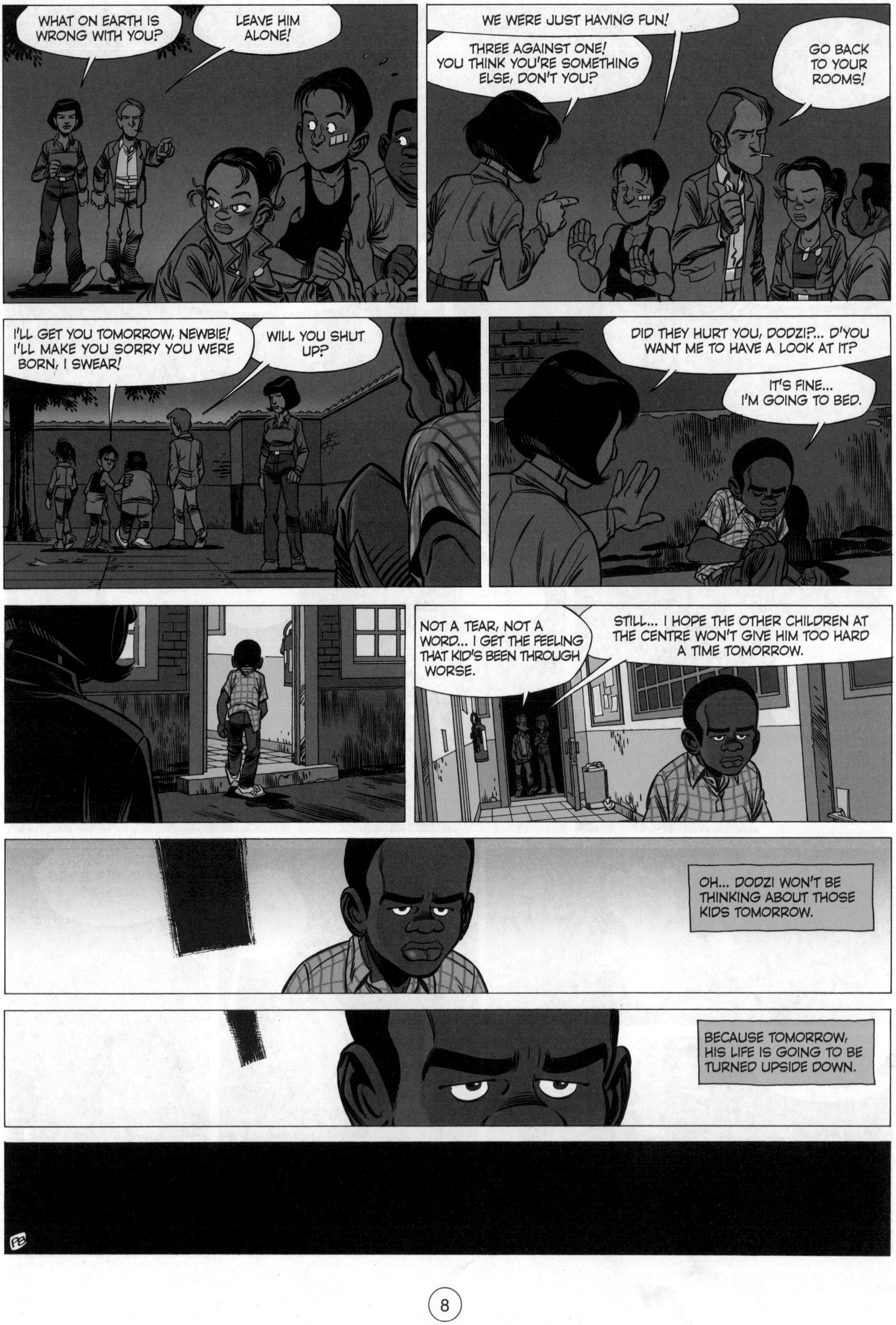
WHAT ON EARTH IS WRONG WITH YOU?
LEAVE HIM ALONE!
WE WERE JUST HAVING FUN!
THREE AGAINST ONE! YOU THINK YOU'RE SOMETHING ELSE, DON'T YOU?
GO BACK TO YOUR ROOMS!
I'LL GET YOU TOMORROW, NEWBIE! I'LL MAKE YOU SORRY YOU WERE BORN, I SWEAR!
WILL YOU SHUT UP?
DID THEY HURT YOU, DODZI?... D'YOU WANT ME TO HAVE A LOOK AT IT?
IT'S FINE... I'M GOING TO BED.
NOT A TEAR, NOT A WORD... I GET THE FEELING THAT KID'S BEEN THROUGH WORSE.
STILL... I HOPE THE OTHER CHILDREN AT THE CENTRE WON'T GIVE HIM TOO HARD A TIME TOMORROW.
OH... DODZI WON'T BE THINKING ABOUT THOSE KIDS TOMORROW.
BECAUSE TOMORROW, HIS LIFE IS GOING TO BE TURNED UPSIDE DOWN.

Gazzotti
Vehlmann

alone

1 The Vanishing

CINEBOOK
The 9th Art Publisher

I'd like to thank Fabien for his patience and encouragement.
Ralph, Caro and Lili for their support and their friendship.
Also Fred, Nath, Mister Hub and the Nyssen gang.
And, of course, thanks to Josephine and Lucie. May they never feel … alone.
Bruno

I want to thank my parents.
Fabien

Original title: Seuls – La disparition
Original edition: © Dupuis, 2006 by Gazzotti & Vehlmann
www.dupuis.com • All rights reserved
English translation: © 2014 Cinebook Ltd
Translator: Jerome Saincantin
Lettering and text layout: Design Amorandi
Printed in Spain by Just Colour Graphic

This edition first published in Great Britain in 2014 by
Cinebook Ltd
56 Beech Avenue
Canterbury, Kent, CT4 7TA
www.cinebook.com
A CIP catalogue record for this book is available from
the British Library • ISBN 978-1-84918-196-9

9th CINEBOOK
The 9th Art Publisher

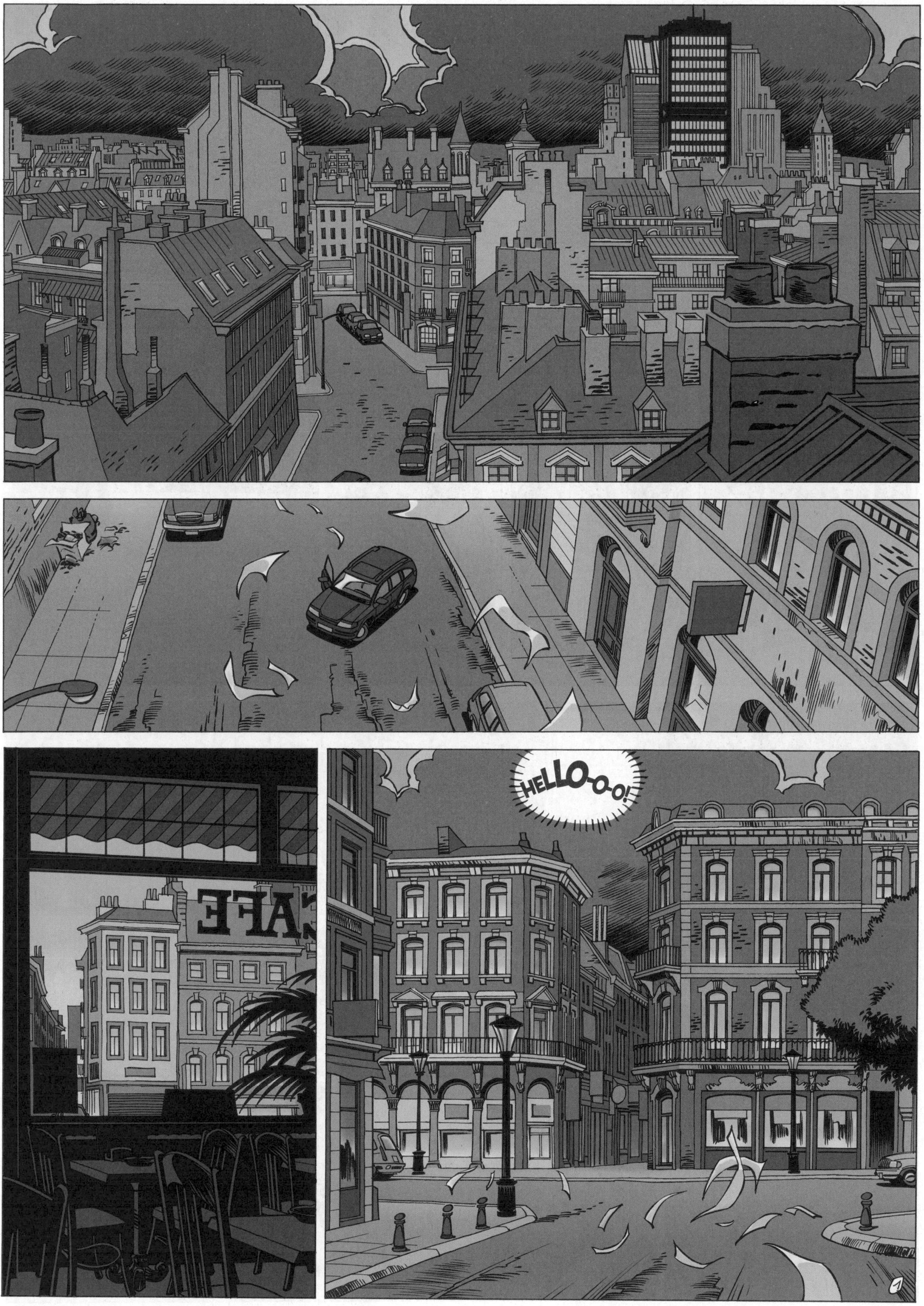
HELLO-O-O!

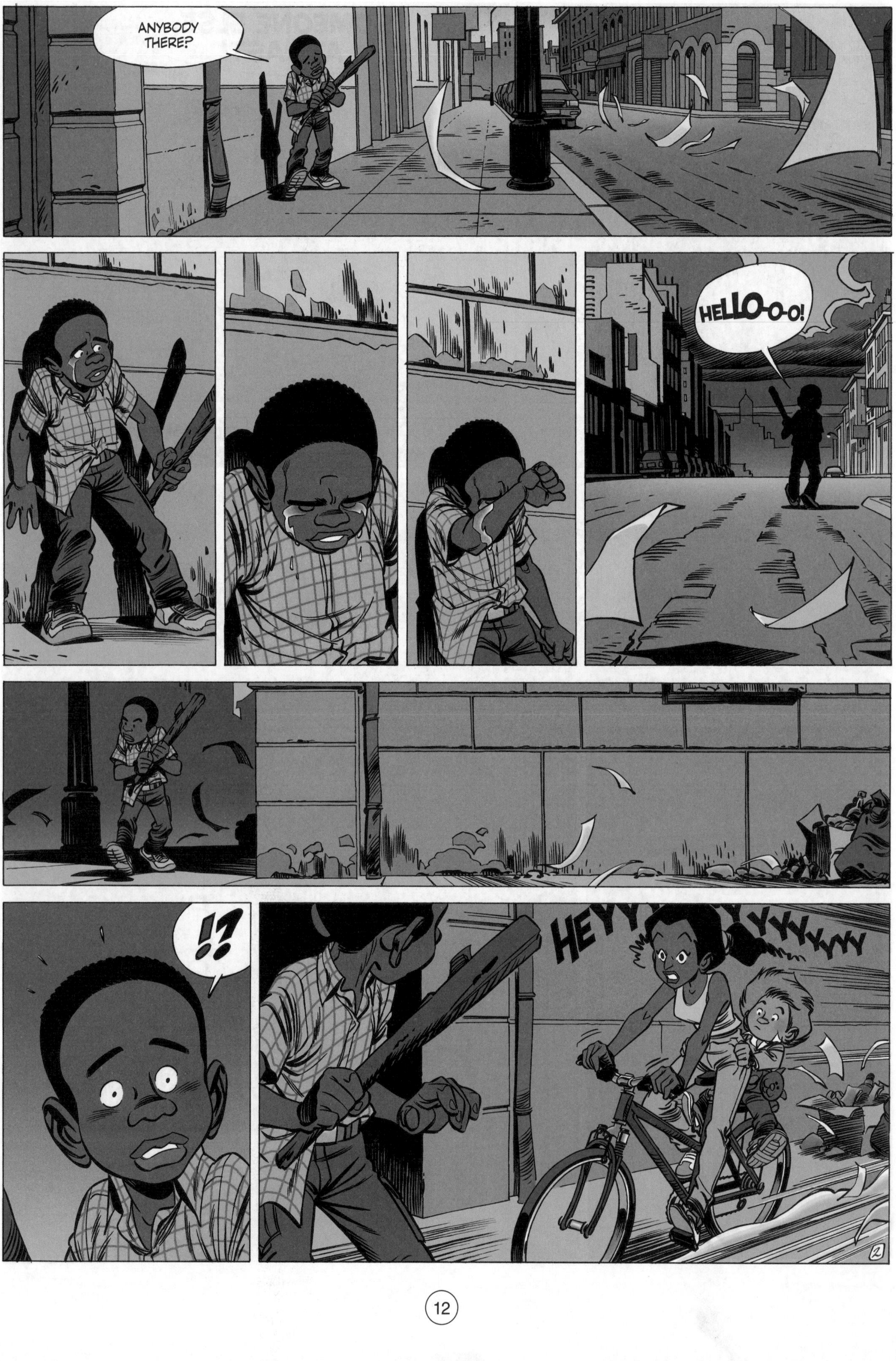
ANYBODY THERE?
HELLO-O-O!
!?
HEYYYYYYYYYY

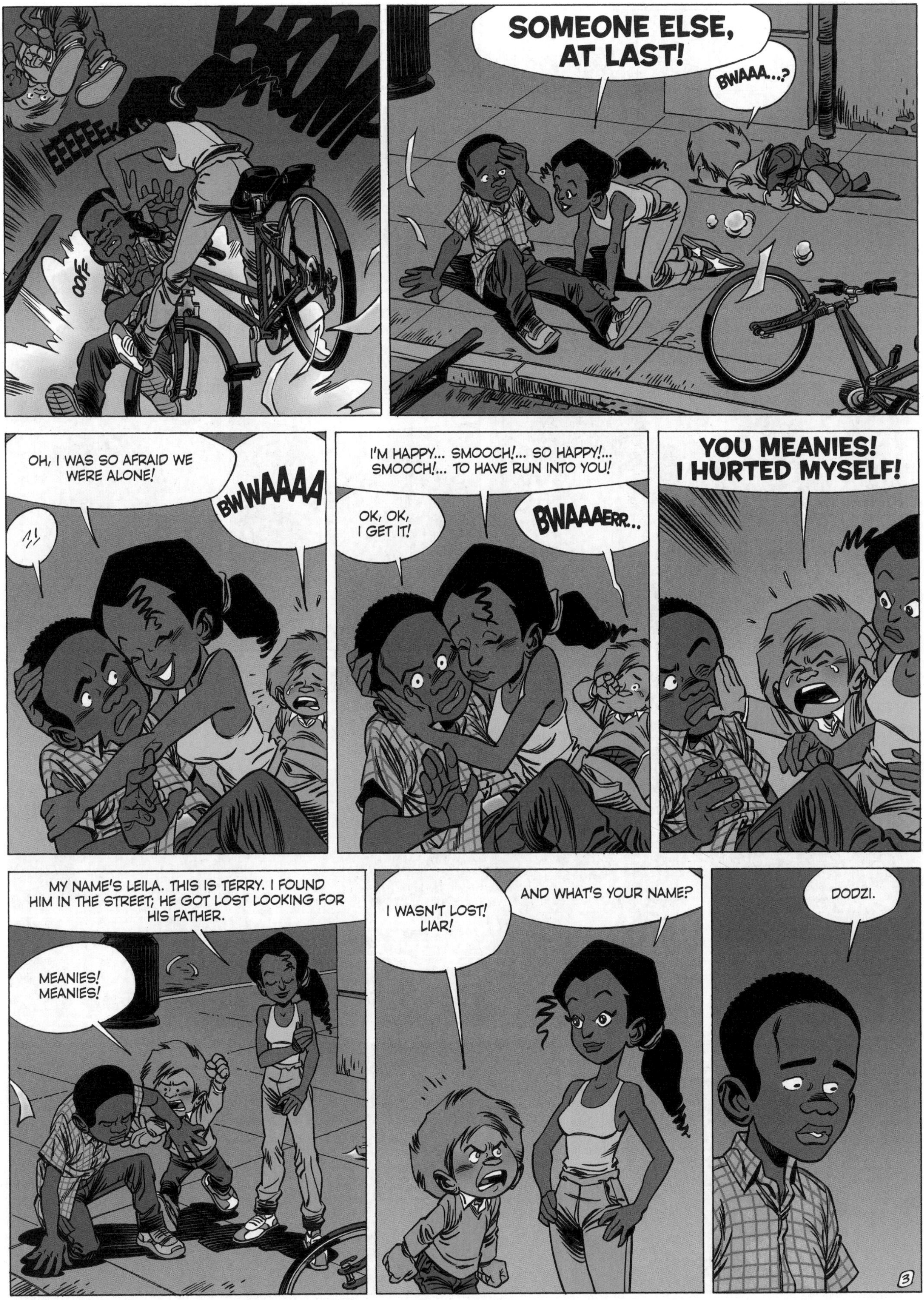
BRROOMP
EEEEEEEK
OOFF
SOMEONE ELSE, AT LAST!
BWAAA...?
OH, I WAS SO AFRAID WE WERE ALONE!
BWWAAAA
I'M HAPPY... SMOOCH!... SO HAPPY!... SMOOCH!... TO HAVE RUN INTO YOU!
OK, OK, I GET IT!
BWAAAERR...
YOU MEANIES! I HURTED MYSELF!
MY NAME'S LEILA. THIS IS TERRY. I FOUND HIM IN THE STREET; HE GOT LOST LOOKING FOR HIS FATHER.
MEANIES! MEANIES!
I WASN'T LOST! LIAR!
AND WHAT'S YOUR NAME?
DODZI.
3

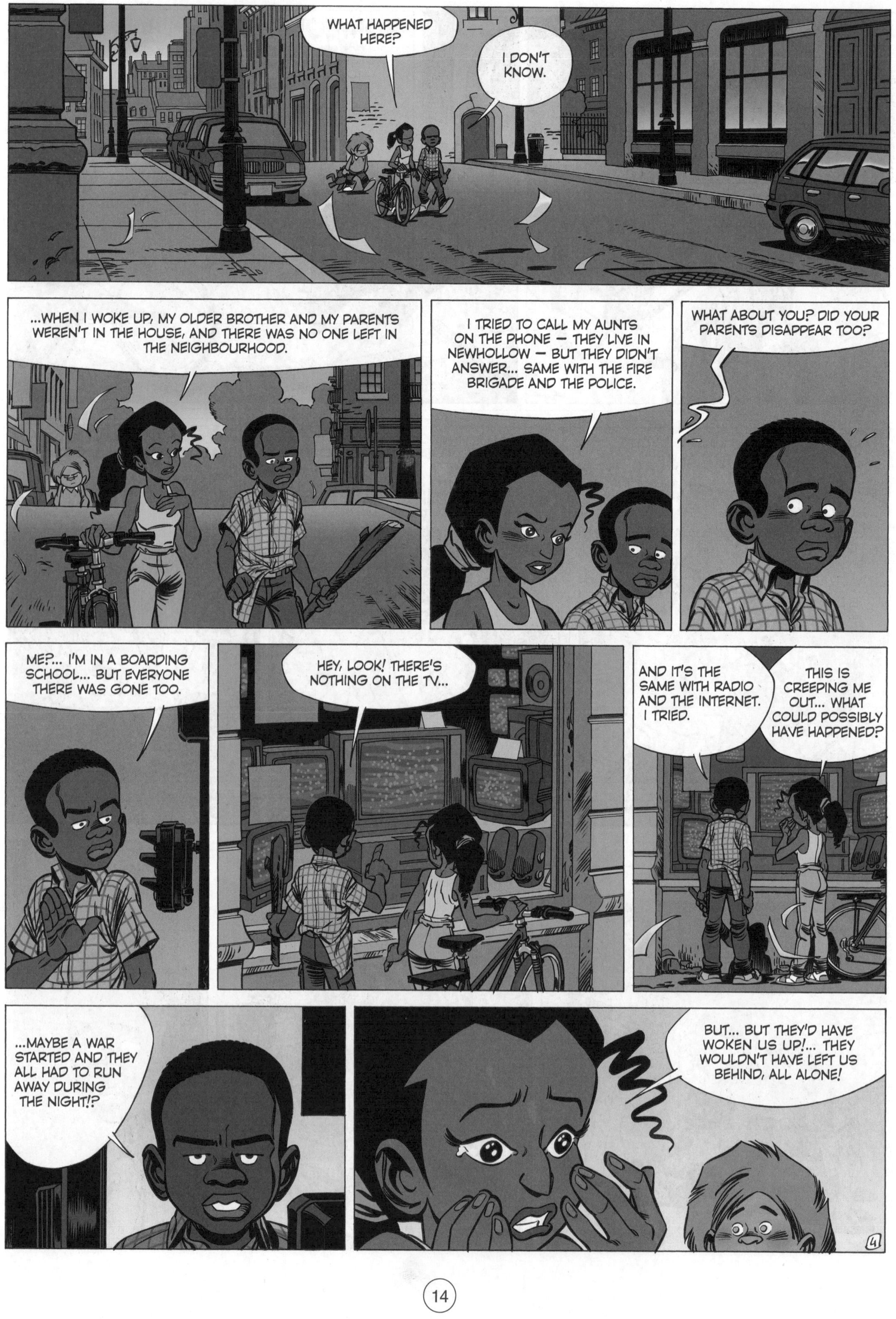
WHAT HAPPENED HERE?
I DON'T KNOW.
...WHEN I WOKE UP, MY OLDER BROTHER AND MY PARENTS WEREN'T IN THE HOUSE, AND THERE WAS NO ONE LEFT IN THE NEIGHBOURHOOD.
I TRIED TO CALL MY AUNTS ON THE PHONE — THEY LIVE IN NEWHOLLOW — BUT THEY DIDN'T ANSWER... SAME WITH THE FIRE BRIGADE AND THE POLICE.
WHAT ABOUT YOU? DID YOUR PARENTS DISAPPEAR TOO?
ME?... I'M IN A BOARDING SCHOOL... BUT EVERYONE THERE WAS GONE TOO.
HEY, LOOK! THERE'S NOTHING ON THE TV...
AND IT'S THE SAME WITH RADIO AND THE INTERNET. I TRIED.
THIS IS CREEPING ME OUT... WHAT COULD POSSIBLY HAVE HAPPENED?
...MAYBE A WAR STARTED AND THEY ALL HAD TO RUN AWAY DURING THE NIGHT!?
BUT... BUT THEY'D HAVE WOKEN US UP!... THEY WOULDN'T HAVE LEFT US BEHIND, ALL ALONE!
4

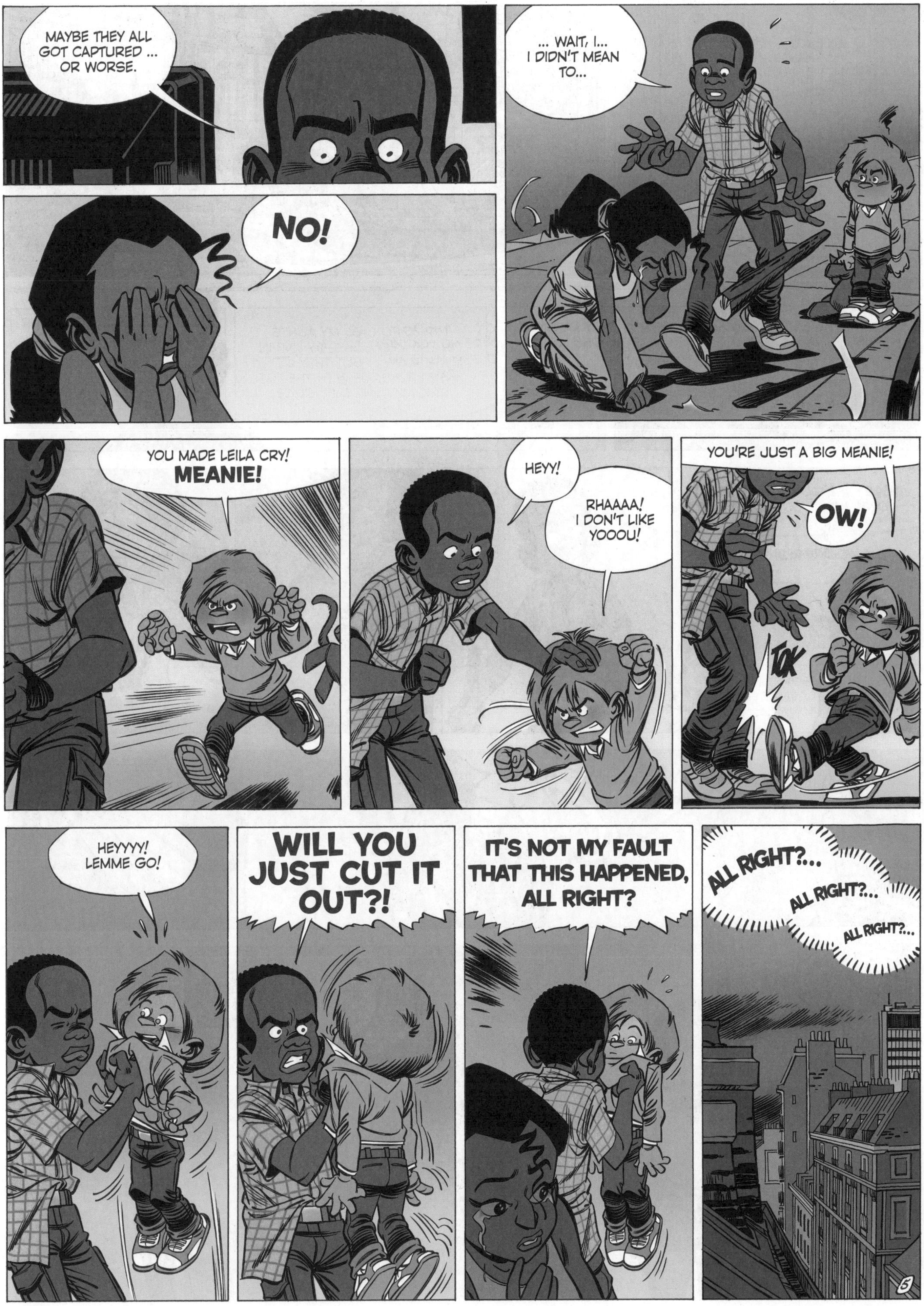
MAYBE THEY ALL GOT CAPTURED ... OR WORSE.
... WAIT, I... I DIDN'T MEAN TO...
NO!
YOU MADE LEILA CRY! MEANIE!
HEYY!
RHAAAA! I DON'T LIKE YOOOU!
YOU'RE JUST A BIG MEANIE!
OW!
TOK
HEYYYY! LEMME GO!
WILL YOU JUST CUT IT OUT?!
IT'S NOT MY FAULT THAT THIS HAPPENED, ALL RIGHT?
ALL RIGHT?...
ALL RIGHT?...
ALL RIGHT?...

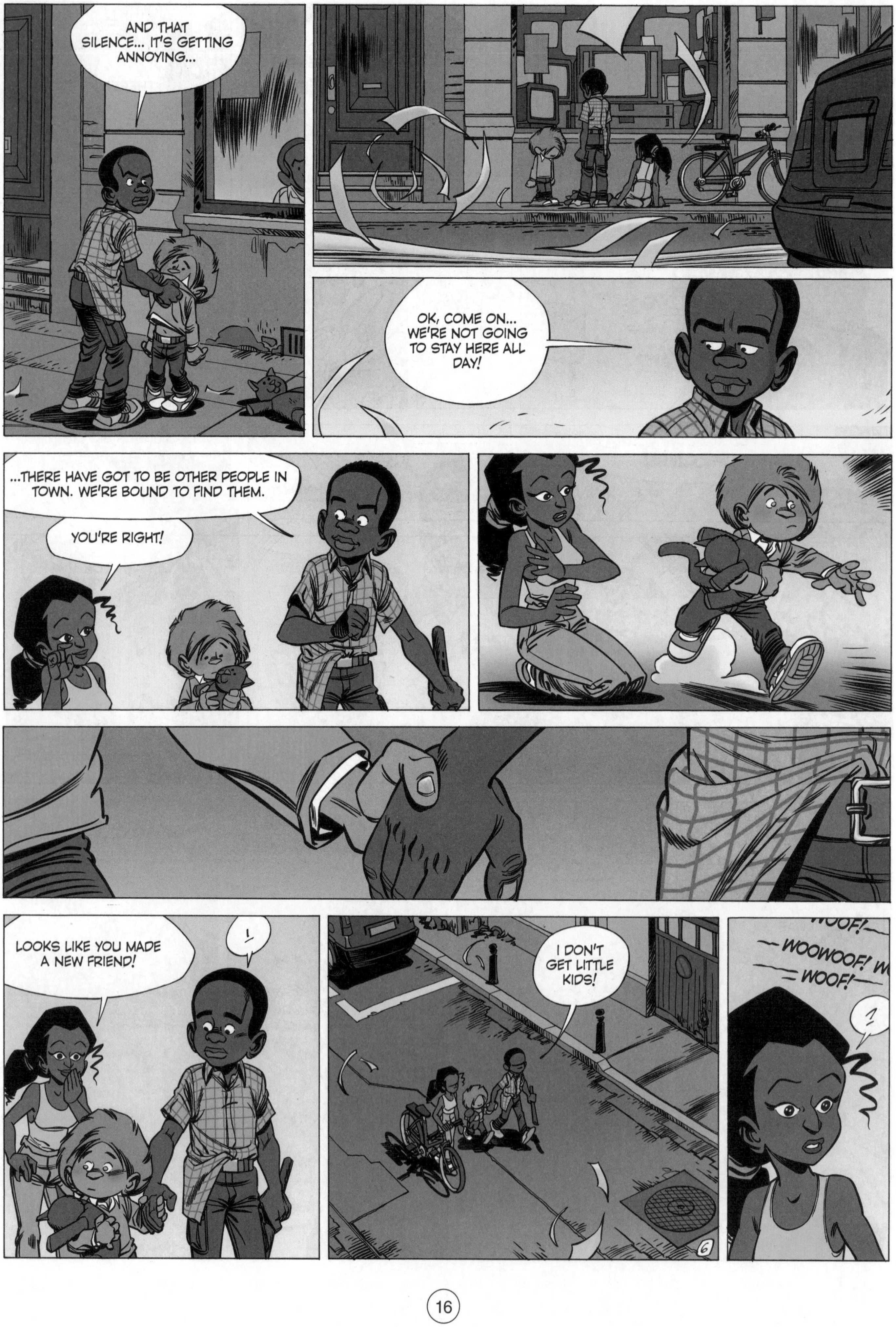
AND THAT SILENCE... IT'S GETTING ANNOYING...
OK, COME ON... WE'RE NOT GOING TO STAY HERE ALL DAY!
...THERE HAVE GOT TO BE OTHER PEOPLE IN TOWN. WE'RE BOUND TO FIND THEM.
YOU'RE RIGHT!
LOOKS LIKE YOU MADE A NEW FRIEND!
!
I DON'T GET LITTLE KIDS!
WOOF!
WOOWOOF!
WOOF!
?

TIN SCHOOL
LEAVE ME ALONE!
WOOF!
WNHOOF
WOOWOOF
WOOF!
LET GO OF MY DRESS! EEEEEEEEK!
RHRR HRHH..RRH
THERE!
GO ON, SCRAM!
WOOFWOOWOOF
OH-H-H! OH-H-H, THANKS!
I'M SO HAPPY TO SEE YOU! I WAS SO SCARED!
IT'S ALL RIGHT: NOW YOU'RE NOT ALONE ANY MORE!
YOU NASTY, STINKING DOGGY!
!

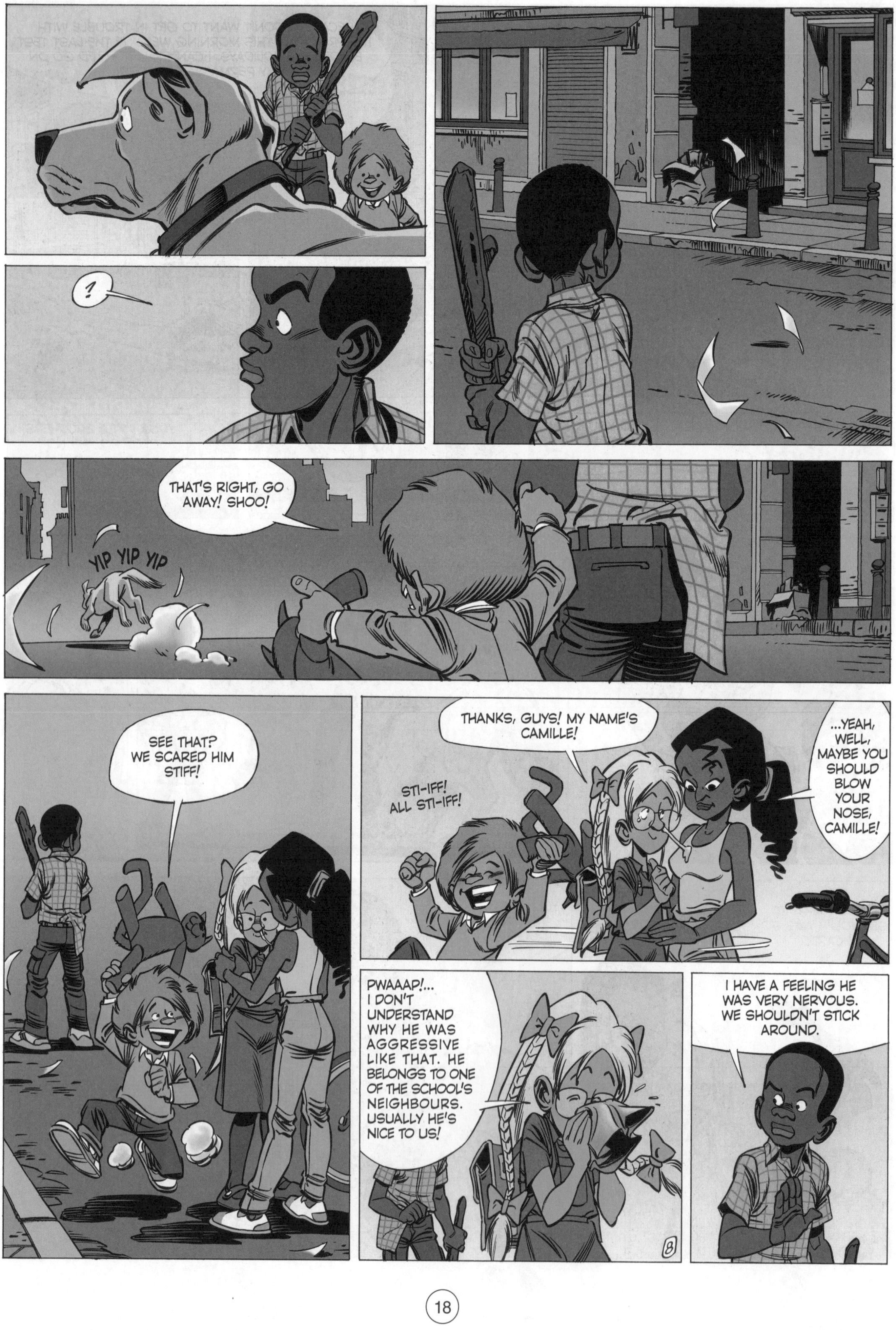
?
THAT'S RIGHT, GO AWAY! SHOO!
YIP YIP YIP
SEE THAT? WE SCARED HIM STIFF!
STI-IFF! ALL STI-IFF!
THANKS, GUYS! MY NAME'S CAMILLE!
...YEAH, WELL, MAYBE YOU SHOULD BLOW YOUR NOSE, CAMILLE!
PWAAAP!... I DON'T UNDERSTAND WHY HE WAS AGGRESSIVE LIKE THAT. HE BELONGS TO ONE OF THE SCHOOL'S NEIGHBOURS. USUALLY HE'S NICE TO US!
I HAVE A FEELING HE WAS VERY NERVOUS. WE SHOULDN'T STICK AROUND.

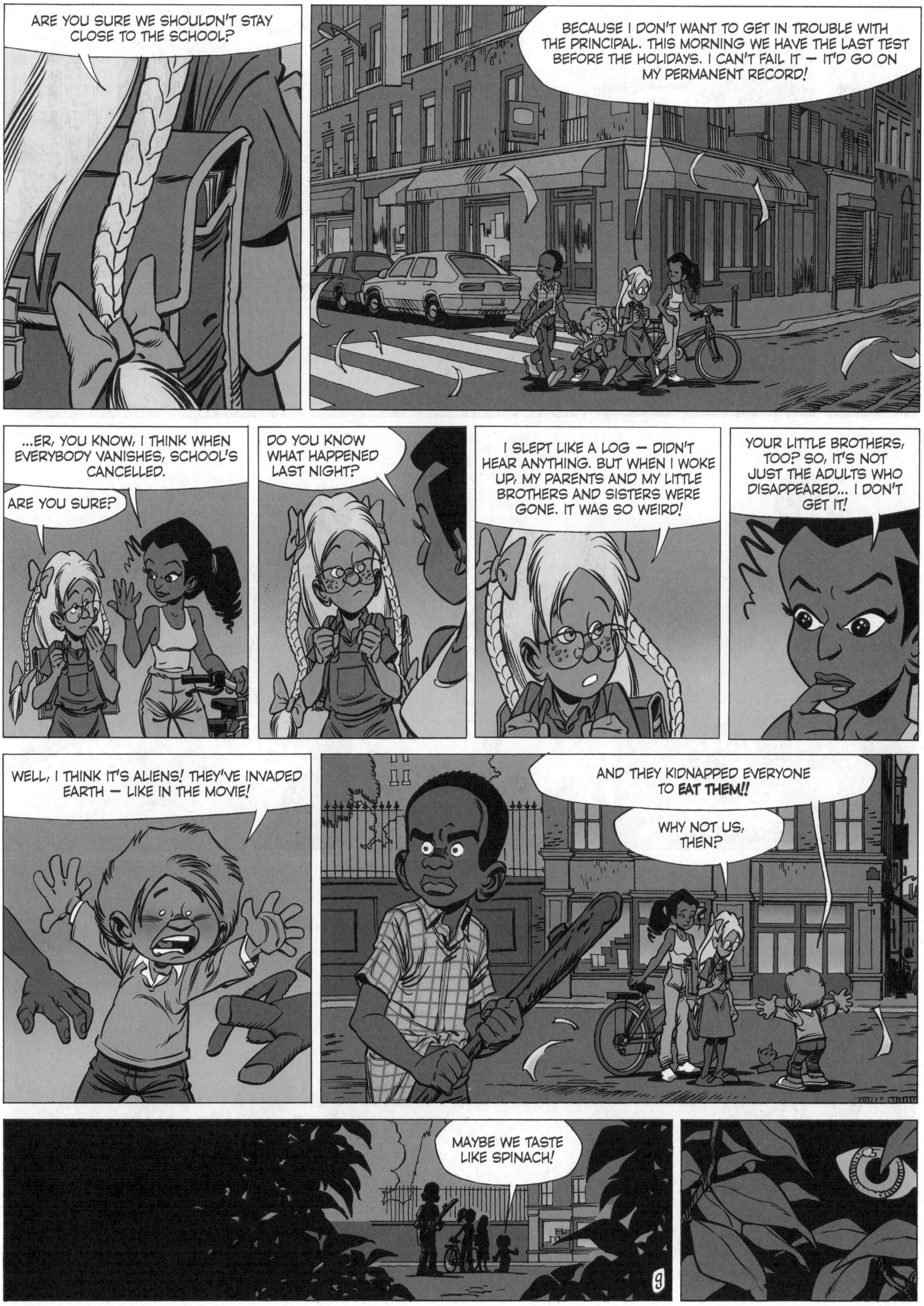
ARE YOU SURE WE SHOULDN'T STAY CLOSE TO THE SCHOOL?
BECAUSE I DON'T WANT TO GET IN TROUBLE WITH THE PRINCIPAL. THIS MORNING WE HAVE THE LAST TEST BEFORE THE HOLIDAYS. I CAN'T FAIL IT — IT'D GO ON MY PERMANENT RECORD!
...ER, YOU KNOW, I THINK WHEN EVERYBODY VANISHES, SCHOOL'S CANCELLED.
ARE YOU SURE?
DO YOU KNOW WHAT HAPPENED LAST NIGHT?
I SLEPT LIKE A LOG — DIDN'T HEAR ANYTHING. BUT WHEN I WOKE UP, MY PARENTS AND MY LITTLE BROTHERS AND SISTERS WERE GONE. IT WAS SO WEIRD!
YOUR LITTLE BROTHERS, TOO? SO, IT'S NOT JUST THE ADULTS WHO DISAPPEARED... I DON'T GET IT!
WELL, I THINK IT'S ALIENS! THEY'VE INVADED EARTH — LIKE IN THE MOVIE!
AND THEY KIDNAPPED EVERYONE TO EAT THEM!!
WHY NOT US, THEN?
MAYBE WE TASTE LIKE SPINACH!

IT'S SO HOT AND STUFFY!...

WHO'S UP FOR A NICE DIP?

OH, YEAAAAAAH!

IN THE FOUNTAIN?... THAT'S NOT ALLOWED!

HEY, TERRY, TAKE OFF YOUR CLOTHES FIRST!

PWOOSH!

IT'S WEIRD THAT THE JETS AREN'T WORKING!

I HOPE WE WON'T GET INTO TROUBLE...

PHEW! THAT FEELS SO GOOD!

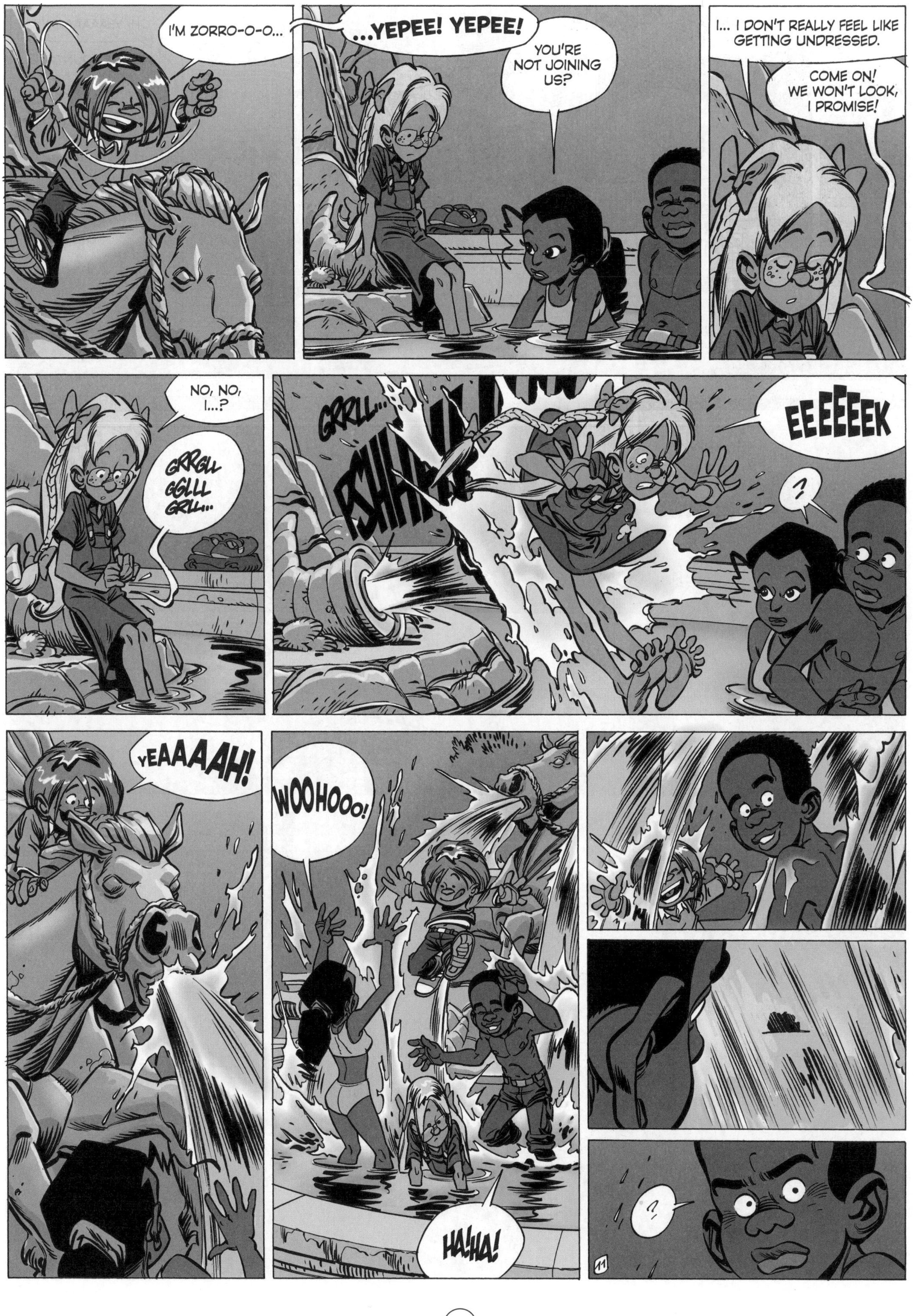
I'M ZORRO-O-O...
...YEPEE! YEPEE!
YOU'RE NOT JOINING US?
I... I DON'T REALLY FEEL LIKE GETTING UNDRESSED.
COME ON! WE WON'T LOOK, I PROMISE!
NO, NO, I...?
GRRGLL GGLLL GRLL...
GRRLL...
FSHHH
EEEEEEK
?
YEAAAAH!
WOOHOOO!
HA!HA!
?
11

ARE YOU LEAVING, DODZI?

...JUST SOMETHING I NEED TO CHECK...

HEY, LEILA!

LOOK, I TOOK OFF MY CLOTHES LIKE YOU SAID!

YOU NITWIT! YOU SHOULD HAVE DONE THAT BEFORE YOU JUMPED IN!

SKRRR...

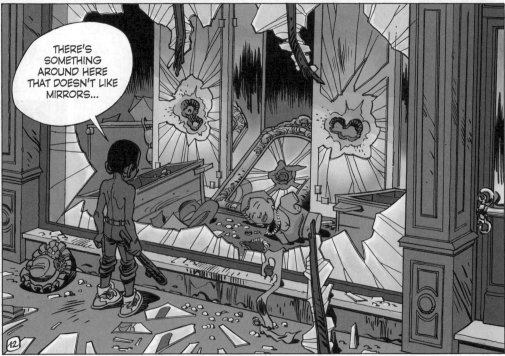

THERE'S SOMETHING AROUND HERE THAT DOESN'T LIKE MIRRORS...

12

22

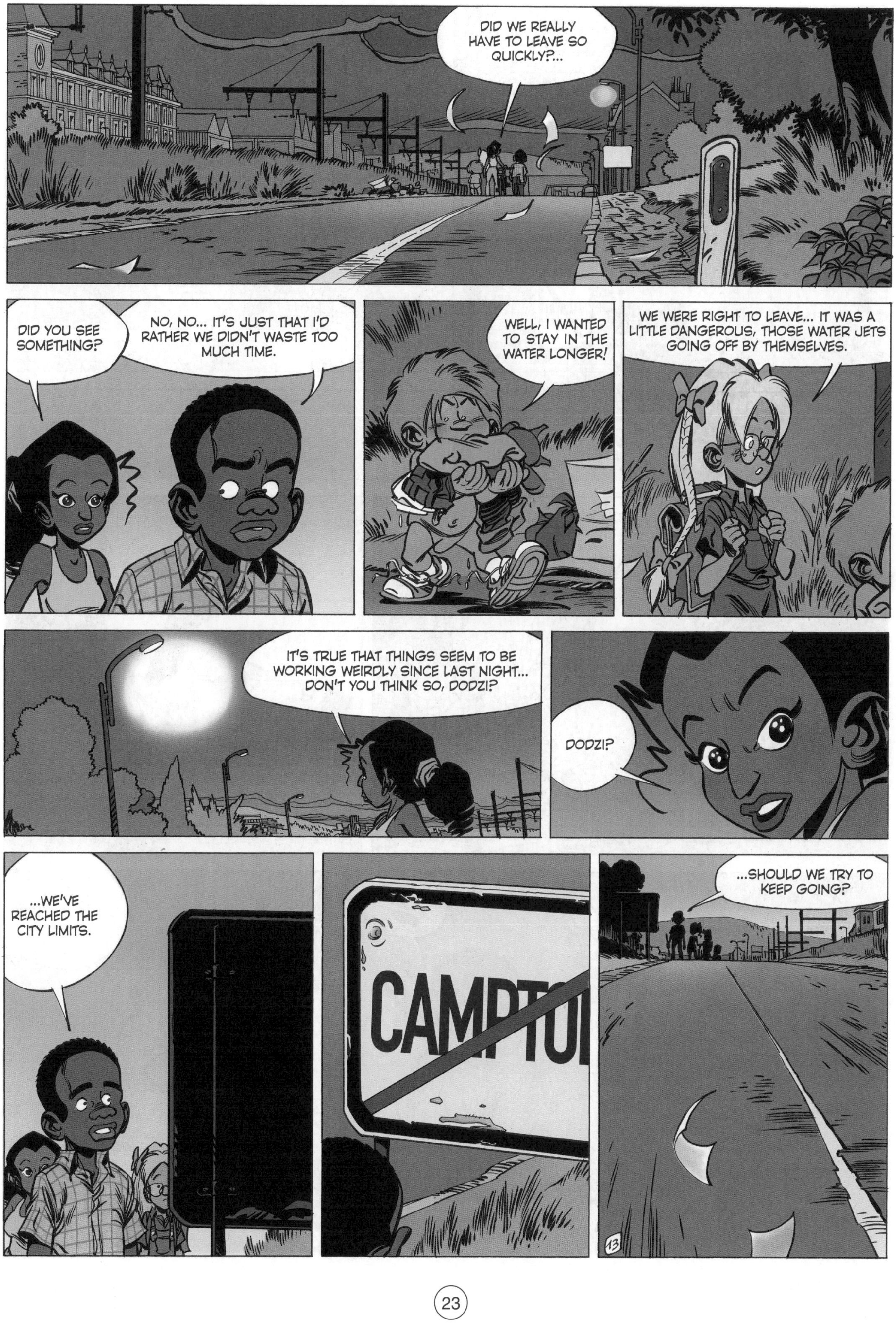
DID WE REALLY HAVE TO LEAVE SO QUICKLY?...
DID YOU SEE SOMETHING?
NO, NO... IT'S JUST THAT I'D RATHER WE DIDN'T WASTE TOO MUCH TIME.
WELL, I WANTED TO STAY IN THE WATER LONGER!
WE WERE RIGHT TO LEAVE... IT WAS A LITTLE DANGEROUS, THOSE WATER JETS GOING OFF BY THEMSELVES.
IT'S TRUE THAT THINGS SEEM TO BE WORKING WEIRDLY SINCE LAST NIGHT... DON'T YOU THINK SO, DODZI?
DODZI?
...WE'VE REACHED THE CITY LIMITS.
CAMPTO
...SHOULD WE TRY TO KEEP GOING?
13

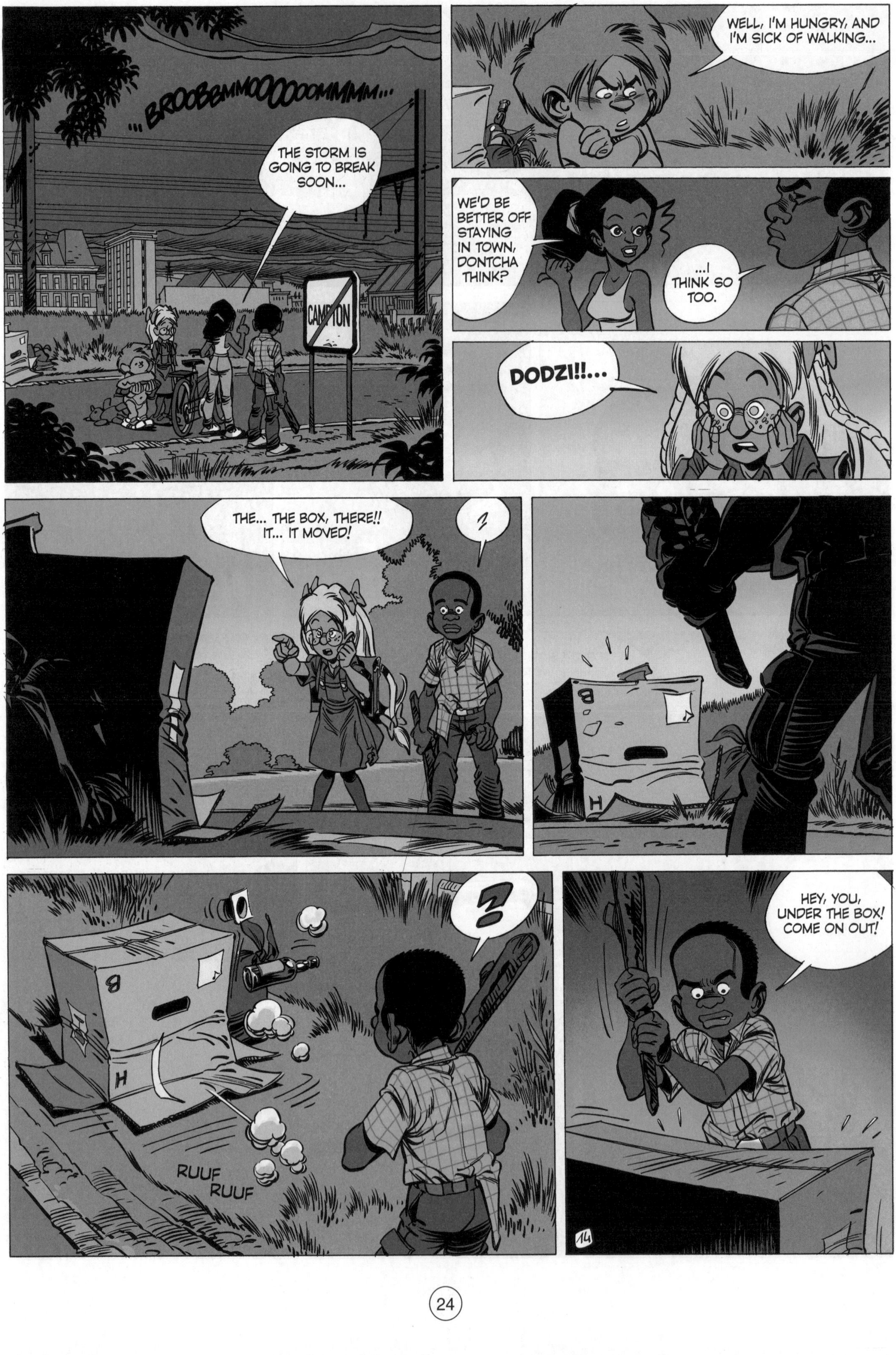
...BROOBBMMOOOOOOMMMM...
THE STORM IS GOING TO BREAK SOON...
CAMPTON
WELL, I'M HUNGRY, AND I'M SICK OF WALKING...
WE'D BE BETTER OFF STAYING IN TOWN, DONTCHA THINK?
...I THINK SO TOO.
DODZI!!!...
THE... THE BOX, THERE!! IT... IT MOVED!
?
?
RUUF RUUF
HEY, YOU, UNDER THE BOX! COME ON OUT!

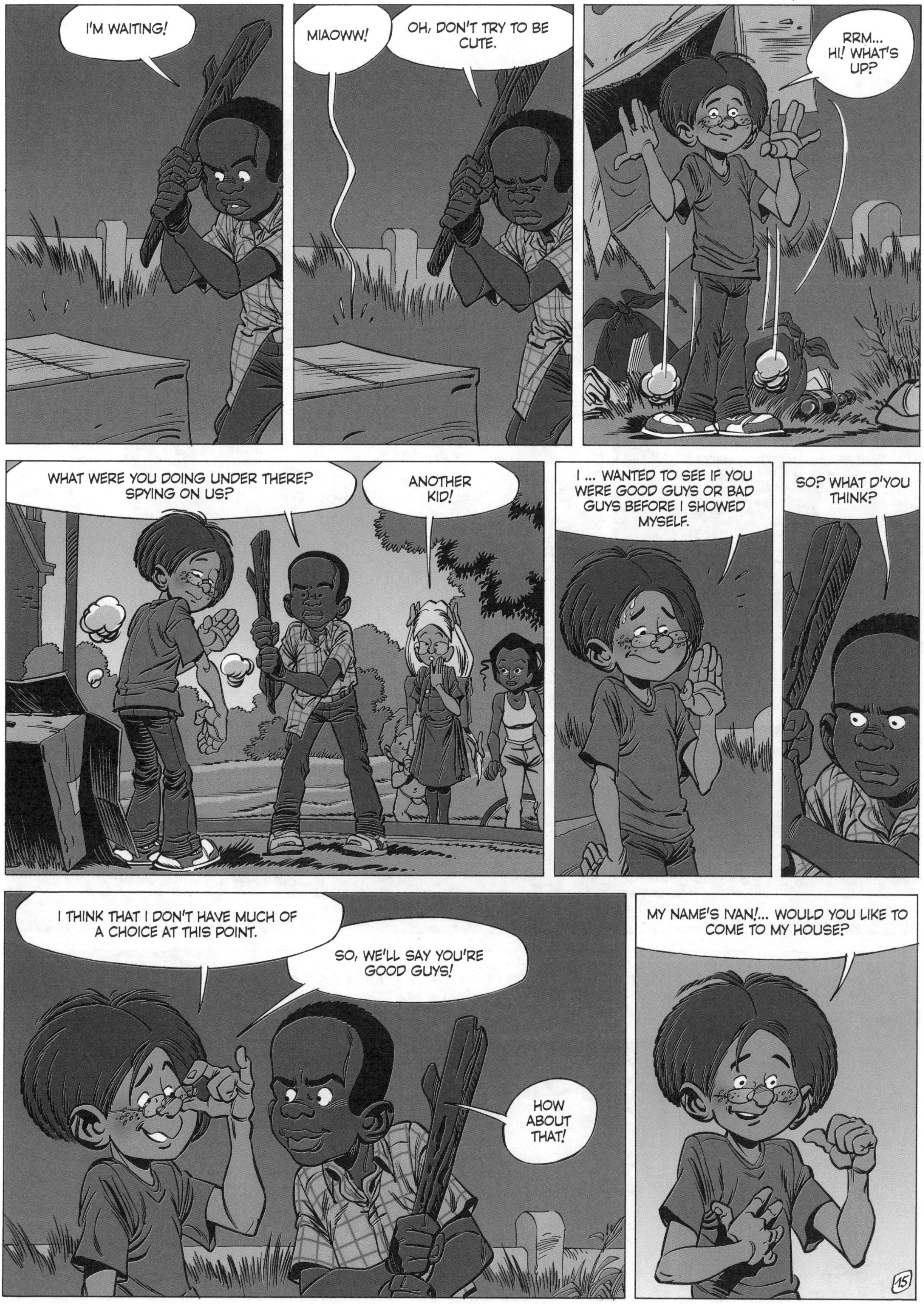
I'M WAITING!
MIAOWW!
OH, DON'T TRY TO BE CUTE.
RRM... HI! WHAT'S UP?
WHAT WERE YOU DOING UNDER THERE? SPYING ON US?
ANOTHER KID!
I ... WANTED TO SEE IF YOU WERE GOOD GUYS OR BAD GUYS BEFORE I SHOWED MYSELF.
SO? WHAT D'YOU THINK?
I THINK THAT I DON'T HAVE MUCH OF A CHOICE AT THIS POINT.
SO, WE'LL SAY YOU'RE GOOD GUYS!
HOW ABOUT THAT!
MY NAME'S IVAN!... WOULD YOU LIKE TO COME TO MY HOUSE?
15

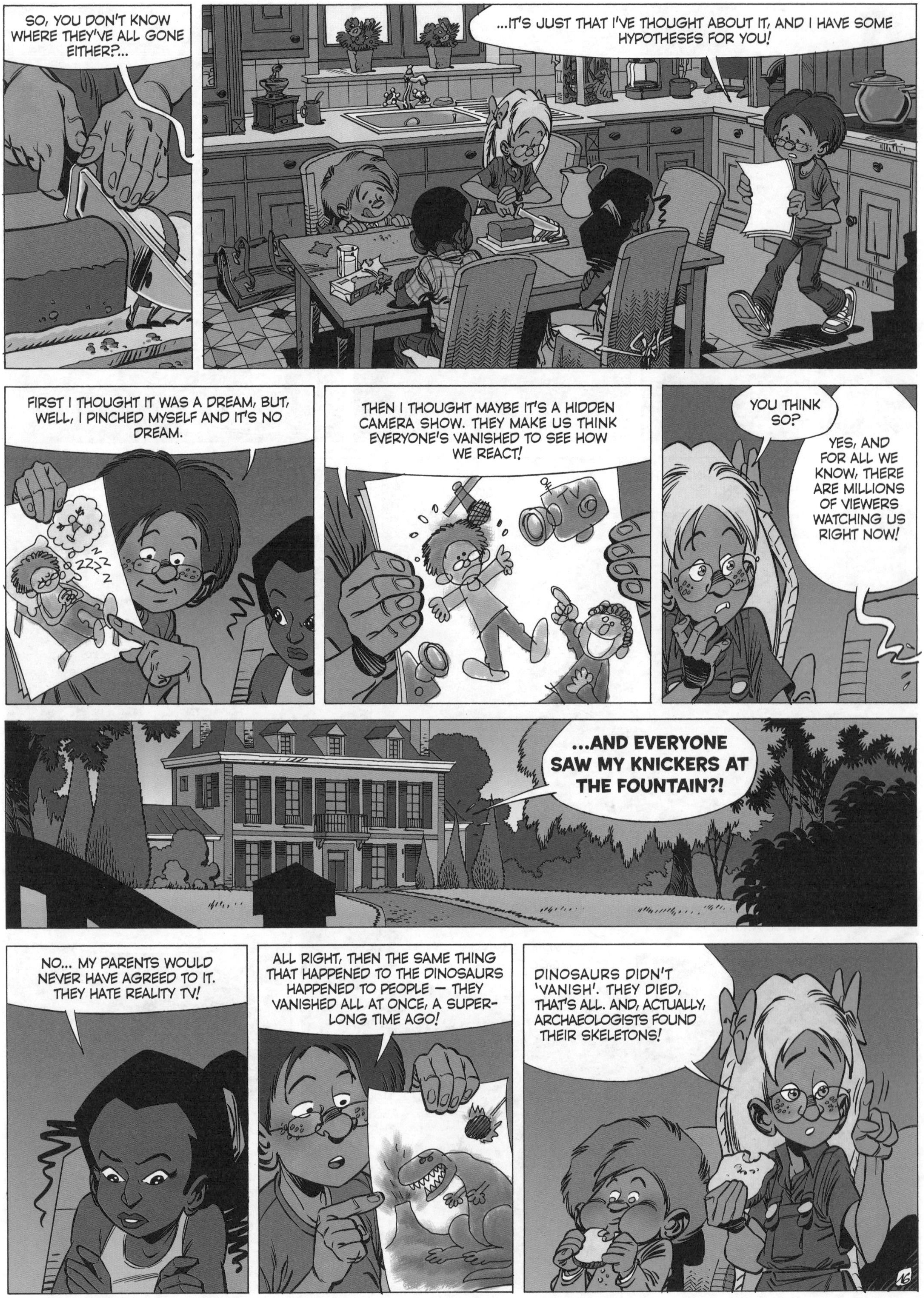
SO, YOU DON'T KNOW WHERE THEY'VE ALL GONE EITHER?...
...IT'S JUST THAT I'VE THOUGHT ABOUT IT, AND I HAVE SOME HYPOTHESES FOR YOU!
FIRST I THOUGHT IT WAS A DREAM, BUT, WELL, I PINCHED MYSELF AND IT'S NO DREAM.
ZZZZ
THEN I THOUGHT MAYBE IT'S A HIDDEN CAMERA SHOW. THEY MAKE US THINK EVERYONE'S VANISHED TO SEE HOW WE REACT!
TV
YOU THINK SO?
YES, AND FOR ALL WE KNOW, THERE ARE MILLIONS OF VIEWERS WATCHING US RIGHT NOW!
...AND EVERYONE SAW MY KNICKERS AT THE FOUNTAIN?!
NO... MY PARENTS WOULD NEVER HAVE AGREED TO IT. THEY HATE REALITY TV!
ALL RIGHT, THEN THE SAME THING THAT HAPPENED TO THE DINOSAURS HAPPENED TO PEOPLE — THEY VANISHED ALL AT ONCE, A SUPER-LONG TIME AGO!
DINOSAURS DIDN'T 'VANISH'. THEY DIED, THAT'S ALL. AND, ACTUALLY, ARCHAEOLOGISTS FOUND THEIR SKELETONS!

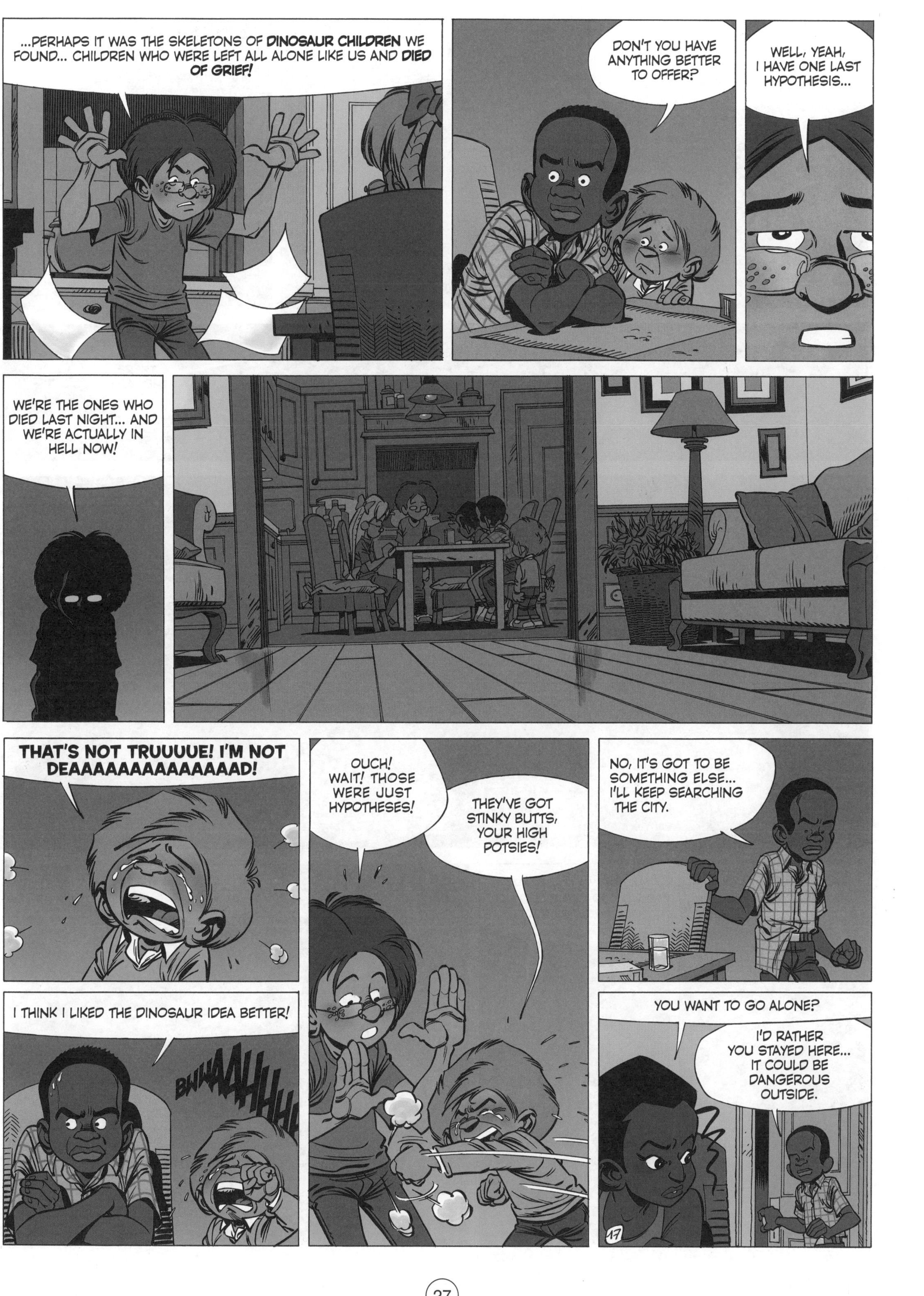
...PERHAPS IT WAS THE SKELETONS OF DINOSAUR CHILDREN WE FOUND... CHILDREN WHO WERE LEFT ALL ALONE LIKE US AND DIED OF GRIEF!
DON'T YOU HAVE ANYTHING BETTER TO OFFER?
WELL, YEAH, I HAVE ONE LAST HYPOTHESIS...
WE'RE THE ONES WHO DIED LAST NIGHT... AND WE'RE ACTUALLY IN HELL NOW!
THAT'S NOT TRUUUUE! I'M NOT DEAAAAAAAAAAAAAAD!
OUCH! WAIT! THOSE WERE JUST HYPOTHESES!
THEY'VE GOT STINKY BUTTS, YOUR HIGH POTSIES!
NO, IT'S GOT TO BE SOMETHING ELSE... I'LL KEEP SEARCHING THE CITY.
I THINK I LIKED THE DINOSAUR IDEA BETTER!
BWAAAHHHH
YOU WANT TO GO ALONE?
I'D RATHER YOU STAYED HERE... IT COULD BE DANGEROUS OUTSIDE.
17

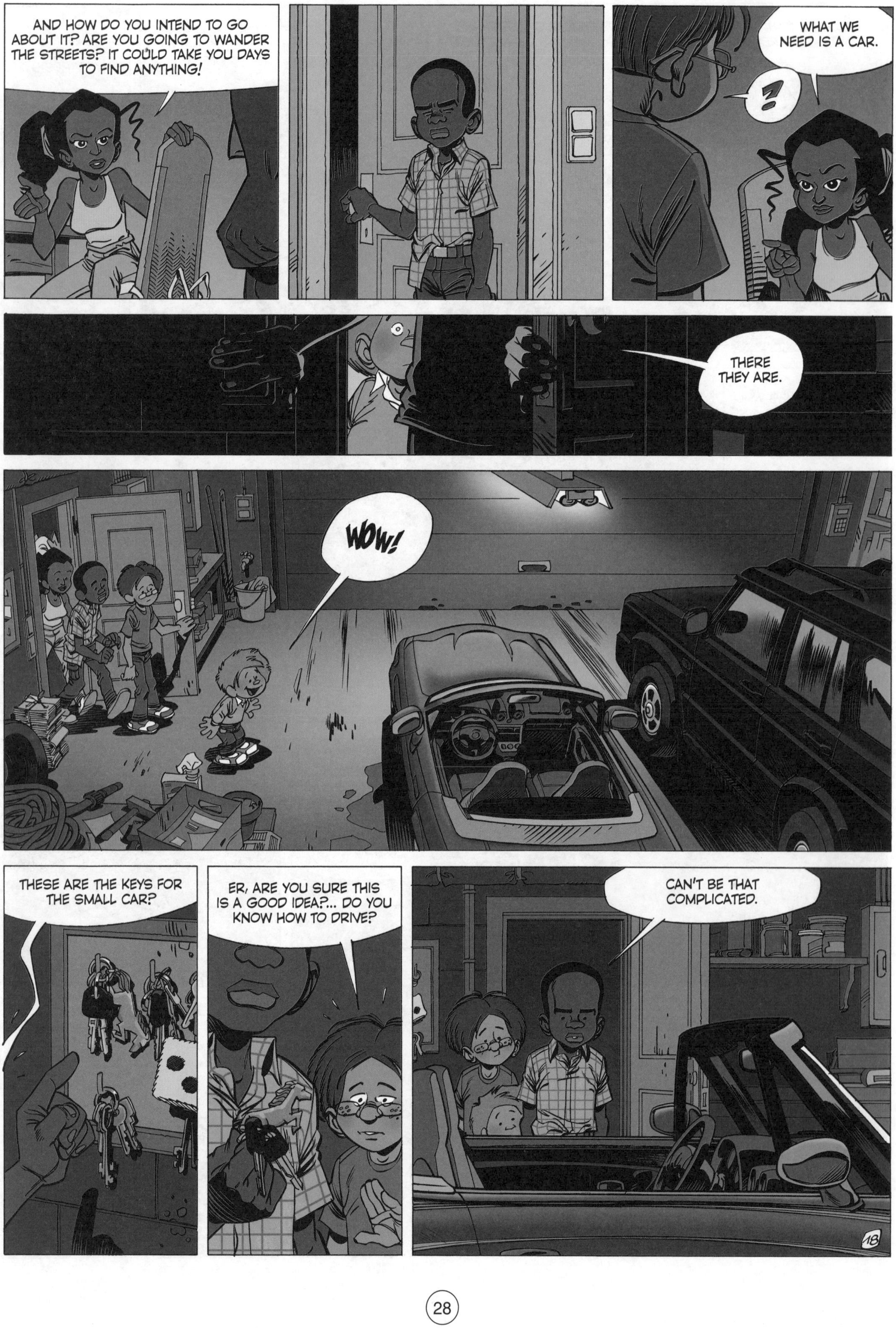

AND HOW DO YOU INTEND TO GO ABOUT IT? ARE YOU GOING TO WANDER THE STREETS? IT COULD TAKE YOU DAYS TO FIND ANYTHING!
WHAT WE NEED IS A CAR.
?
THERE THEY ARE.
WOW!
THESE ARE THE KEYS FOR THE SMALL CAR?
ER, ARE YOU SURE THIS IS A GOOD IDEA?... DO YOU KNOW HOW TO DRIVE?
CAN'T BE THAT COMPLICATED.
18

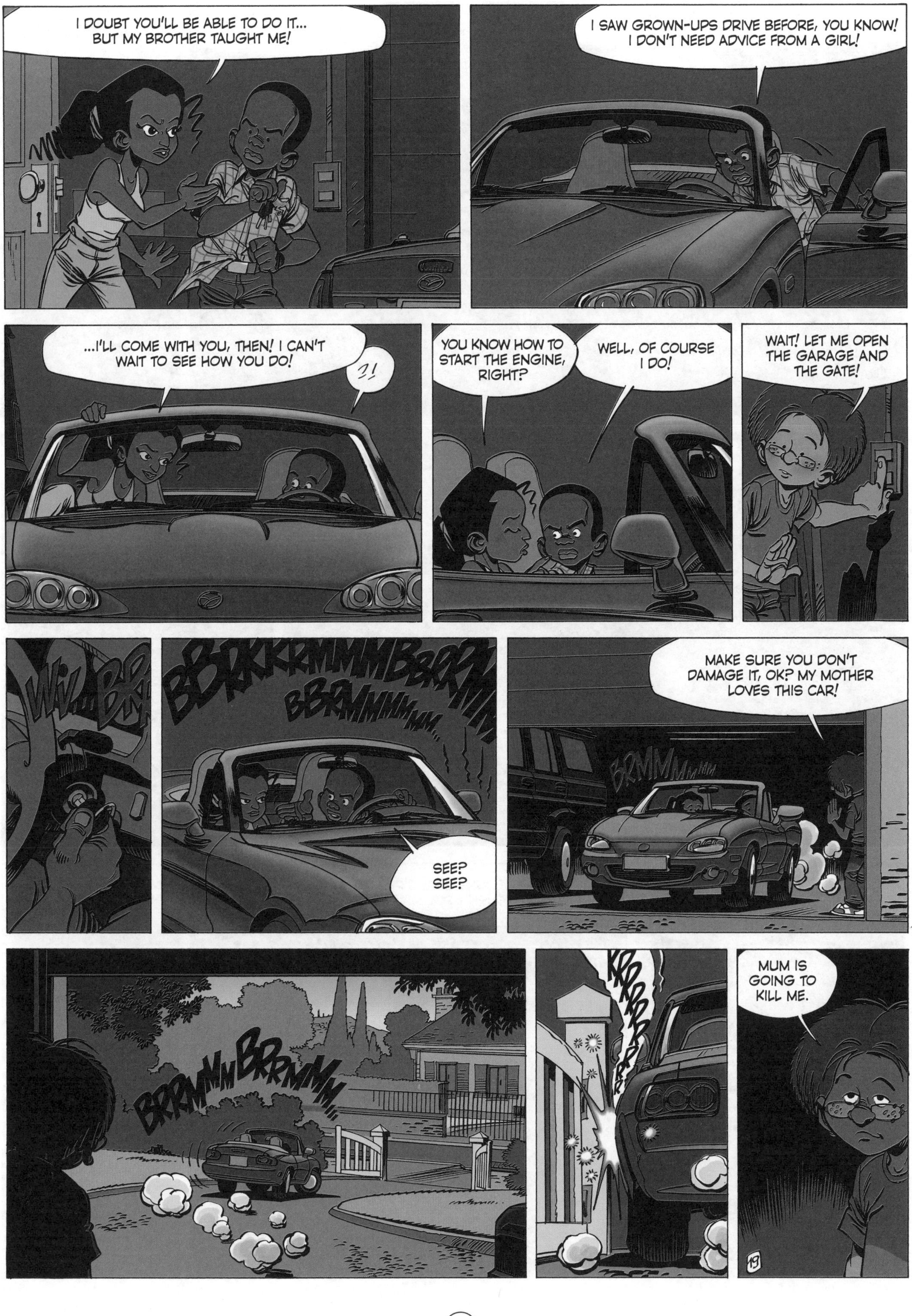

I DOUBT YOU'LL BE ABLE TO DO IT... BUT MY BROTHER TAUGHT ME!
I SAW GROWN-UPS DRIVE BEFORE, YOU KNOW! I DON'T NEED ADVICE FROM A GIRL!
...I'LL COME WITH YOU, THEN! I CAN'T WAIT TO SEE HOW YOU DO!
?!
YOU KNOW HOW TO START THE ENGINE, RIGHT?
WELL, OF COURSE I DO!
WAIT! LET ME OPEN THE GARAGE AND THE GATE!
BBRRKKRMMMBBRRMM
BBRRMMMMMM
SEE? SEE?
MAKE SURE YOU DON'T DAMAGE IT, OK? MY MOTHER LOVES THIS CAR!
BRMMMMMM
BRRMMMBRRMMM
KRRRRRRR
MUM IS GOING TO KILL ME.

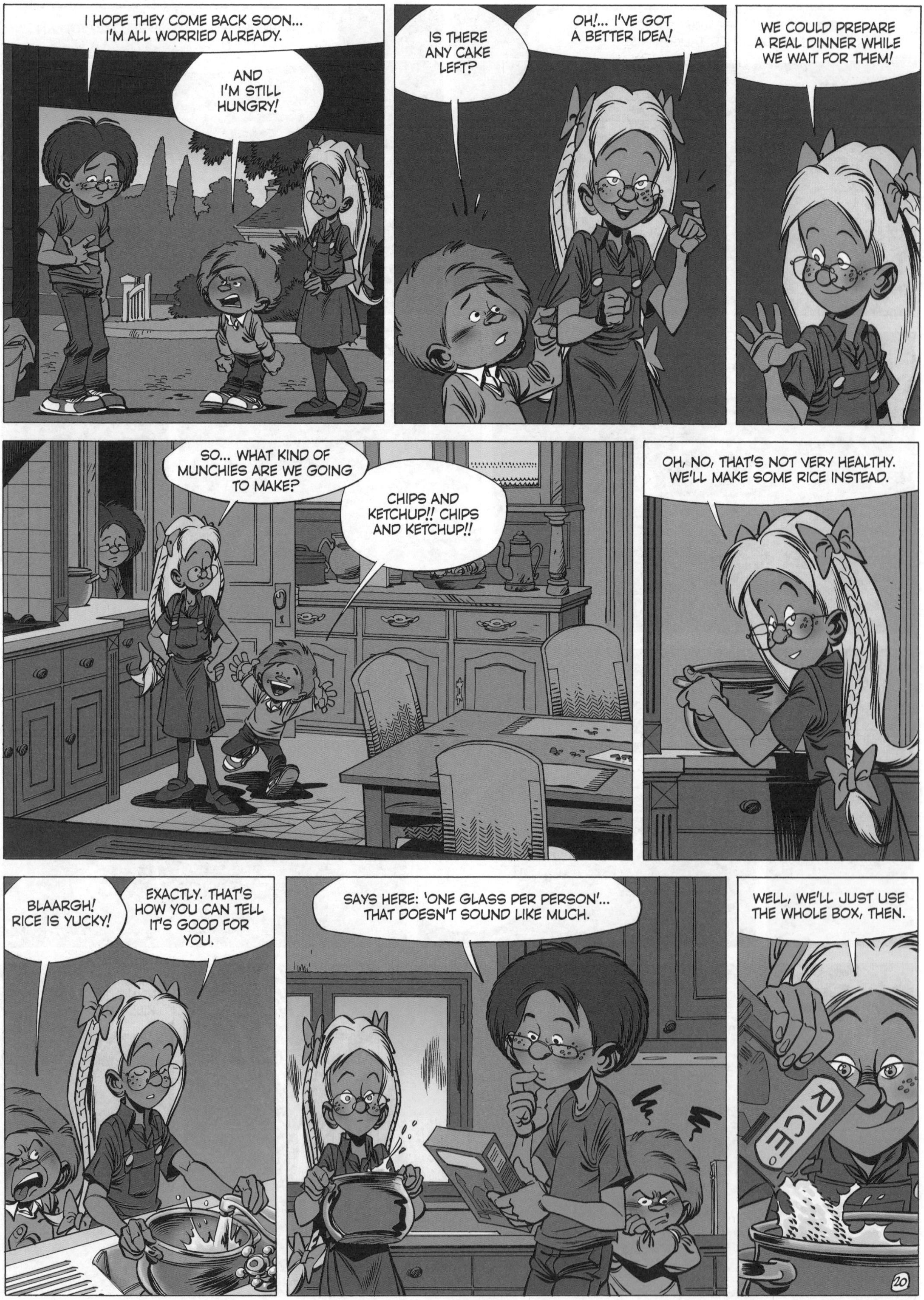
I HOPE THEY COME BACK SOON... I'M ALL WORRIED ALREADY.
AND I'M STILL HUNGRY!
IS THERE ANY CAKE LEFT?
OH!... I'VE GOT A BETTER IDEA!
WE COULD PREPARE A REAL DINNER WHILE WE WAIT FOR THEM!
SO... WHAT KIND OF MUNCHIES ARE WE GOING TO MAKE?
CHIPS AND KETCHUP!! CHIPS AND KETCHUP!!
OH, NO, THAT'S NOT VERY HEALTHY. WE'LL MAKE SOME RICE INSTEAD.
BLAARGH! RICE IS YUCKY!
EXACTLY. THAT'S HOW YOU CAN TELL IT'S GOOD FOR YOU.
SAYS HERE: 'ONE GLASS PER PERSON'... THAT DOESN'T SOUND LIKE MUCH.
WELL, WE'LL JUST USE THE WHOLE BOX, THEN.
RICE
20

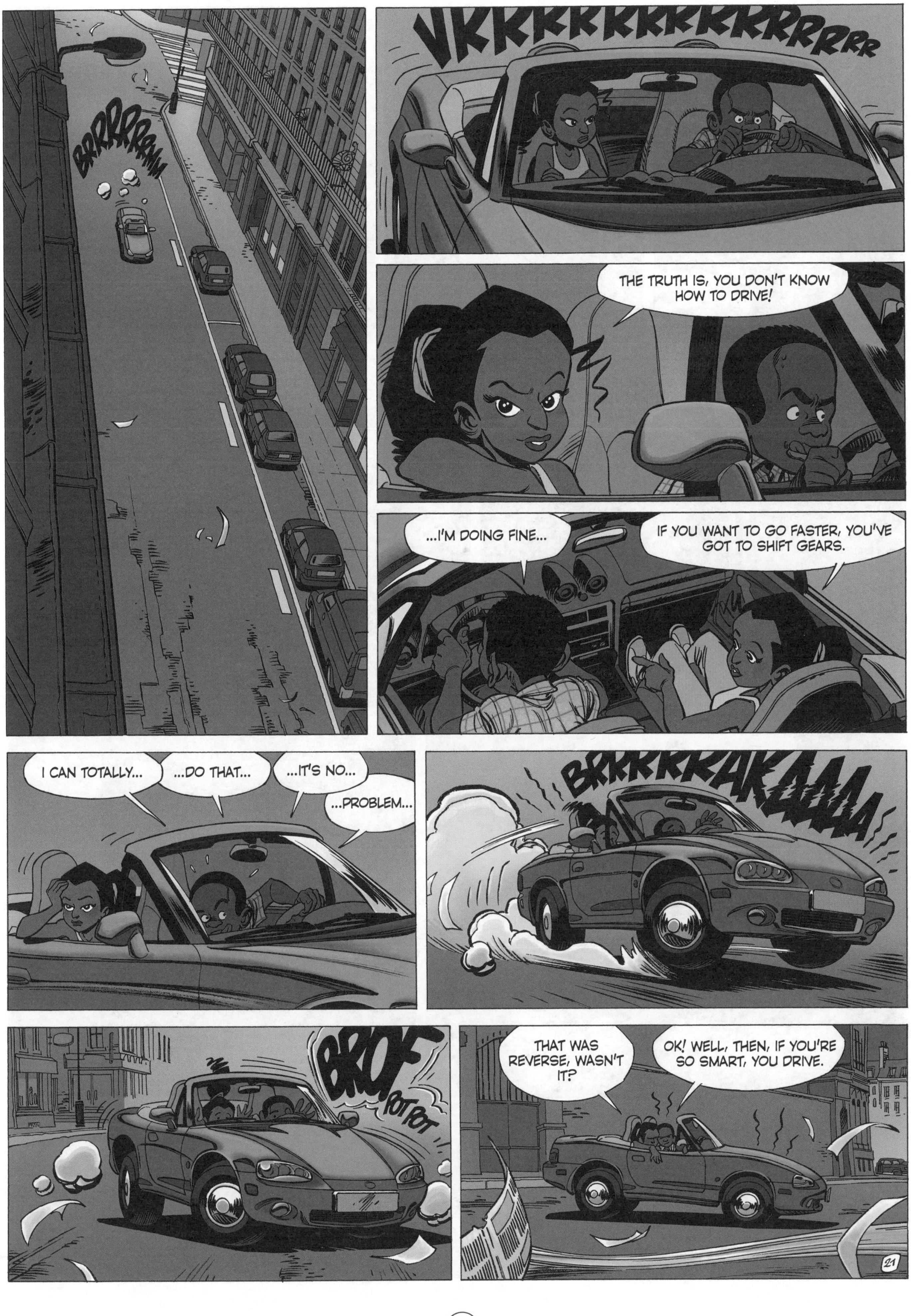
BRRRRRRAMM
VKKKKKKKKKKKRRRRR
THE TRUTH IS, YOU DON'T KNOW HOW TO DRIVE!
...I'M DOING FINE...
IF YOU WANT TO GO FASTER, YOU'VE GOT TO SHIFT GEARS.
I CAN TOTALLY...
...DO THAT...
...IT'S NO...
...PROBLEM...
BRRRRRAKAAAAA
BROF
POT POT
THAT WAS REVERSE, WASN'T IT?
OK! WELL, THEN, IF YOU'RE SO SMART, YOU DRIVE.
21

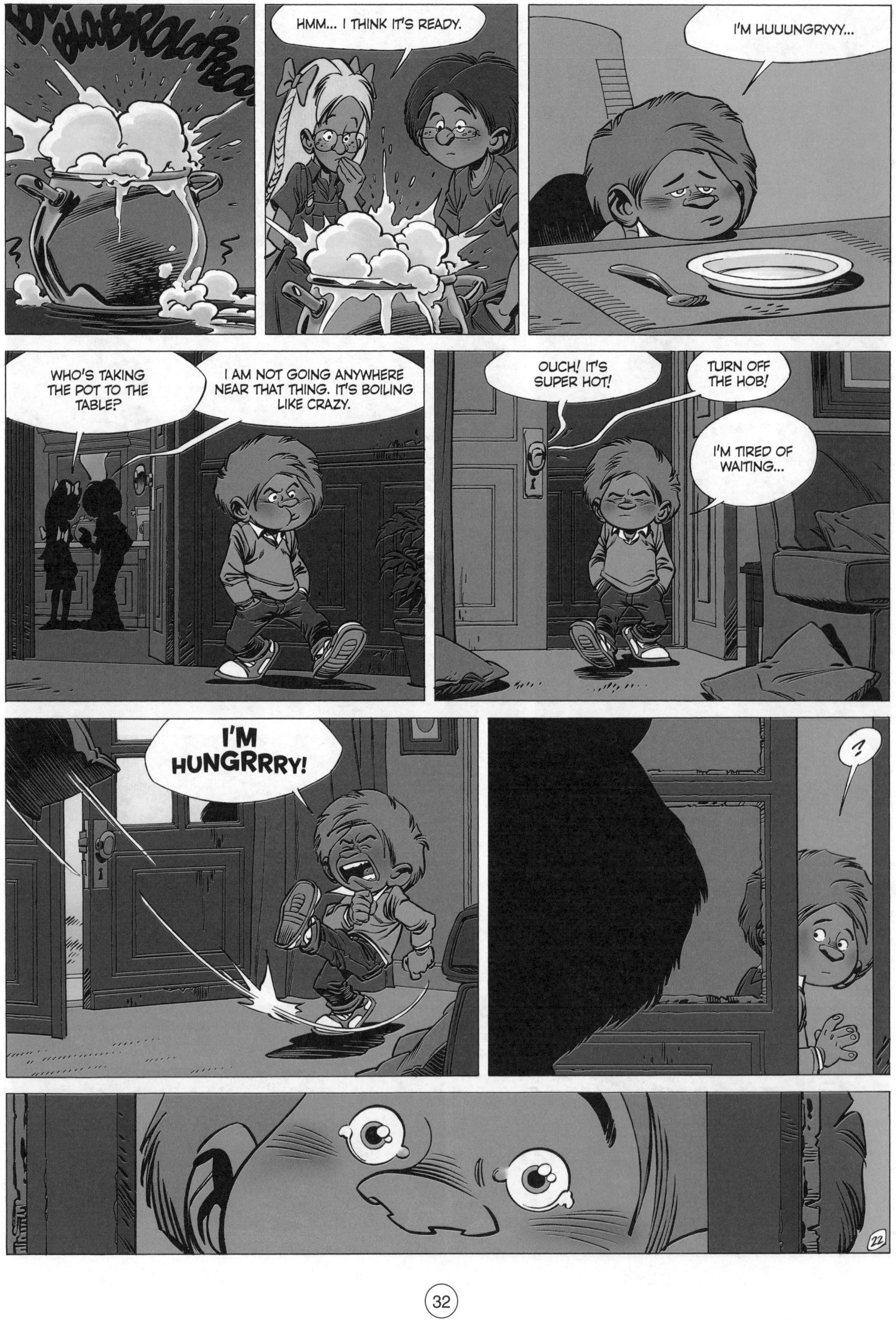
HMM... I THINK IT'S READY.
I'M HUUUNGRYYY...
WHO'S TAKING THE POT TO THE TABLE?
I AM NOT GOING ANYWHERE NEAR THAT THING. IT'S BOILING LIKE CRAZY.
OUCH! IT'S SUPER HOT!
TURN OFF THE HOB!
I'M TIRED OF WAITING...
I'M HUNGRRRY!
?

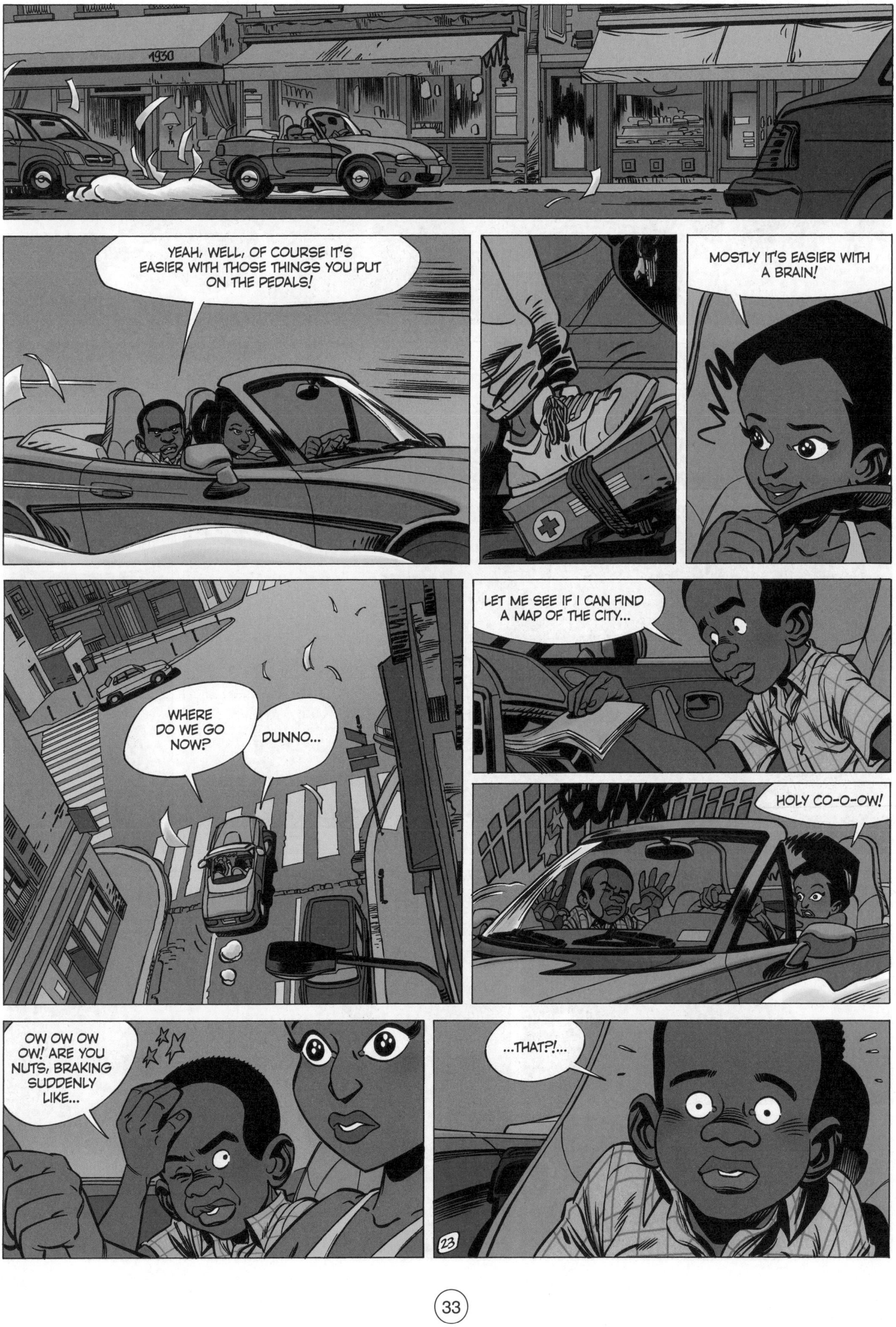
1930
YEAH, WELL, OF COURSE IT'S EASIER WITH THOSE THINGS YOU PUT ON THE PEDALS!
MOSTLY IT'S EASIER WITH A BRAIN!
WHERE DO WE GO NOW?
DUNNO...
LET ME SEE IF I CAN FIND A MAP OF THE CITY...
BUNK
HOLY CO-O-OW!
OW OW OW OW! ARE YOU NUTS, BRAKING SUDDENLY LIKE...
...THAT?!...
23

YOU HAVE GOT TO BE FREAKING KIDDING ME?!

SO, THAT'S WHAT BROKE THE SHOP WINDOW!...

BUT, WHERE DID THEY COME FROM? THERE ISN'T EVEN A ZOO IN CAMPTON!

I'LL HONK TO SCARE THEM AWAY!

THAT'S NOT A GOOD IDEA!

... AAAAHH, THEY'RE MOVING!

34

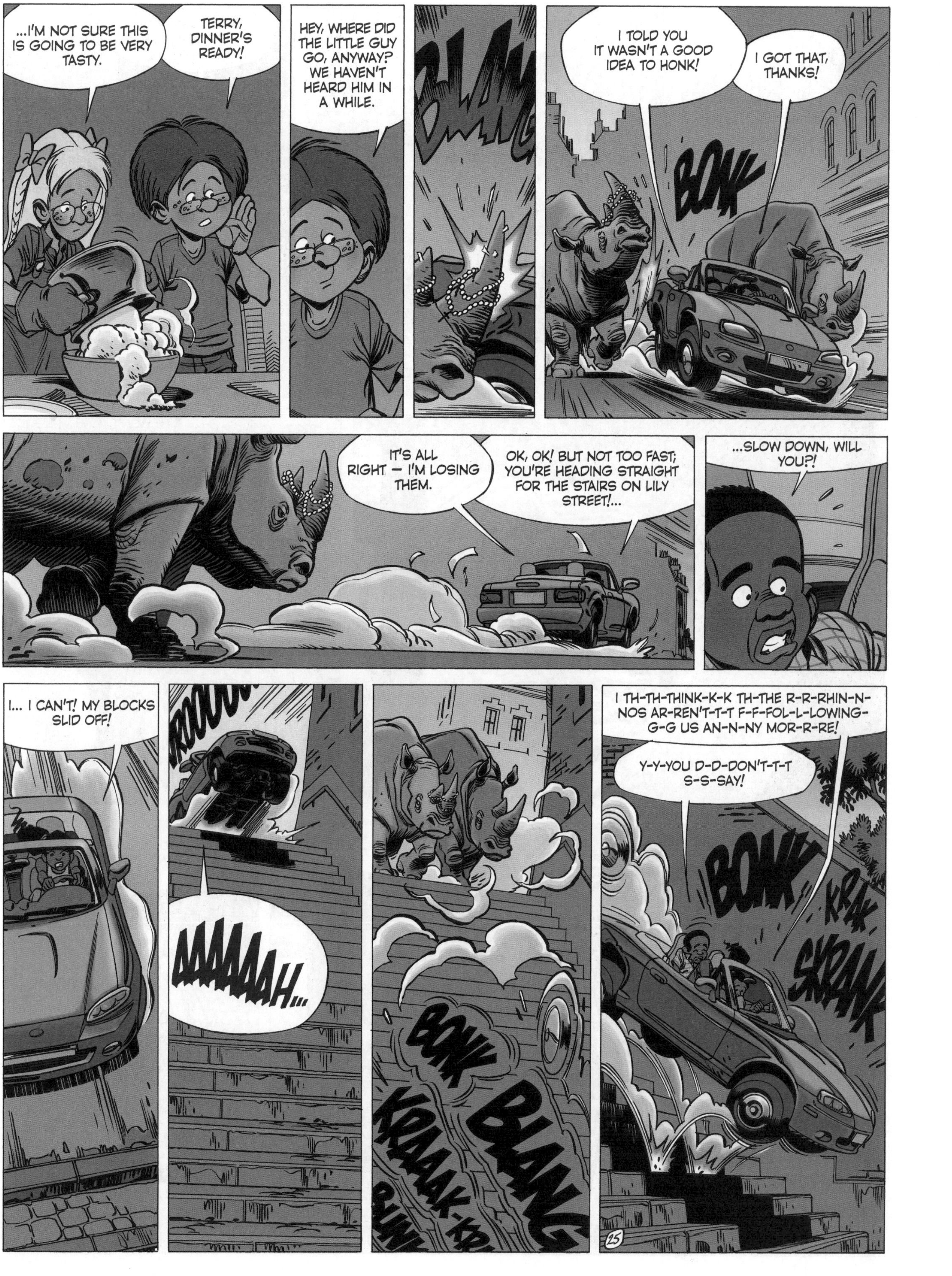
...I'M NOT SURE THIS IS GOING TO BE VERY TASTY.
TERRY, DINNER'S READY!
HEY, WHERE DID THE LITTLE GUY GO, ANYWAY? WE HAVEN'T HEARD HIM IN A WHILE.
BLANG
I TOLD YOU IT WASN'T A GOOD IDEA TO HONK!
I GOT THAT, THANKS!
BONK
IT'S ALL RIGHT – I'M LOSING THEM.
OK, OK! BUT NOT TOO FAST; YOU'RE HEADING STRAIGHT FOR THE STAIRS ON LILY STREET!...
...SLOW DOWN, WILL YOU?!
I... I CAN'T! MY BLOCKS SLID OFF!
AAAAAAAH...
BONK
BLANG
KRAAAK-KRAK
I TH-TH-THINK-K-K TH-THE R-R-RHIN-N-NOS AR-REN'T-T-T F-F-FOL-L-LOWING-G-G US AN-N-NY MOR-R-RE!
Y-Y-YOU D-D-DON'T-T-T S-S-SAY!
BONK
KRAK
SKRANK
25

TERRY?...
YOU MUSTN'T BE AFRAID, ALL RIGHT?
TERRY, COME BACK TOWARDS US.
HE WON'T MOVE... HE'S TOO SCARED... AND I'M RIGHT THERE WITH HIM!
I'LL GO AND GET HIM.
TERRY?
COME ON — WE CAN'T STAY HERE.
26

VRRRRRRR...
THE CAR!... THE OTHERS ARE BACK!
BWWAAAH!
QUICK, TO THE GARAGE!
YOU WON'T BELIEVE WHAT WE SAW!
GOTTA CLOSE THE GARAGE, NOWWWWW!
PAK
SLAM
KLAK
IT WAS HORRIBLE! THAT... THAT AWFUL ANIMAL!
...ENORMOUS RHINOCE-ROSES!...
THE MONSTER WANTED TO EAT MEEEEE!
IT WAS A TIGER, BUT ALL WEIRD! AND HE MIGHT BE INSIDE THE HOUSE: THE LIVING ROOM WINDOW'S OPEN!
I DON'T LIKE THIS! I'M SCARED!
WHAT? WE'RE STUCK INSIDE THIS GARAGE? ...
WHY THE HECK DID YOU LEAVE THAT WINDOW OPEN?!
HEY, GET OFF MY BACK!

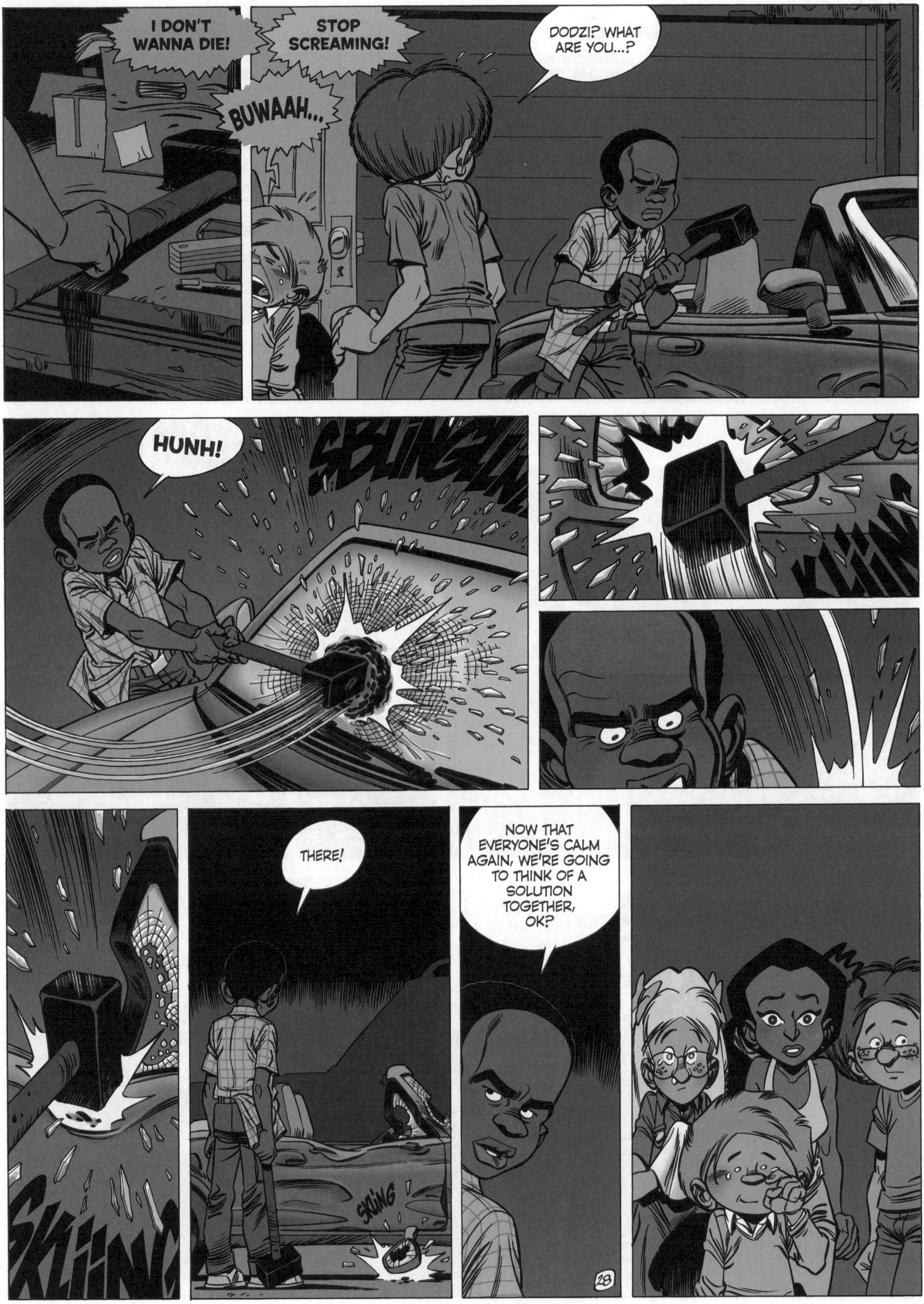
I DON'T WANNA DIE!
STOP SCREAMING!
BUWAAH...
DODZI? WHAT ARE YOU...?
HUNH!
SBLING
KLING
THERE!
SKLING
NOW THAT EVERYONE'S CALM AGAIN, WE'RE GOING TO THINK OF A SOLUTION TOGETHER, OK?
SKLING
28

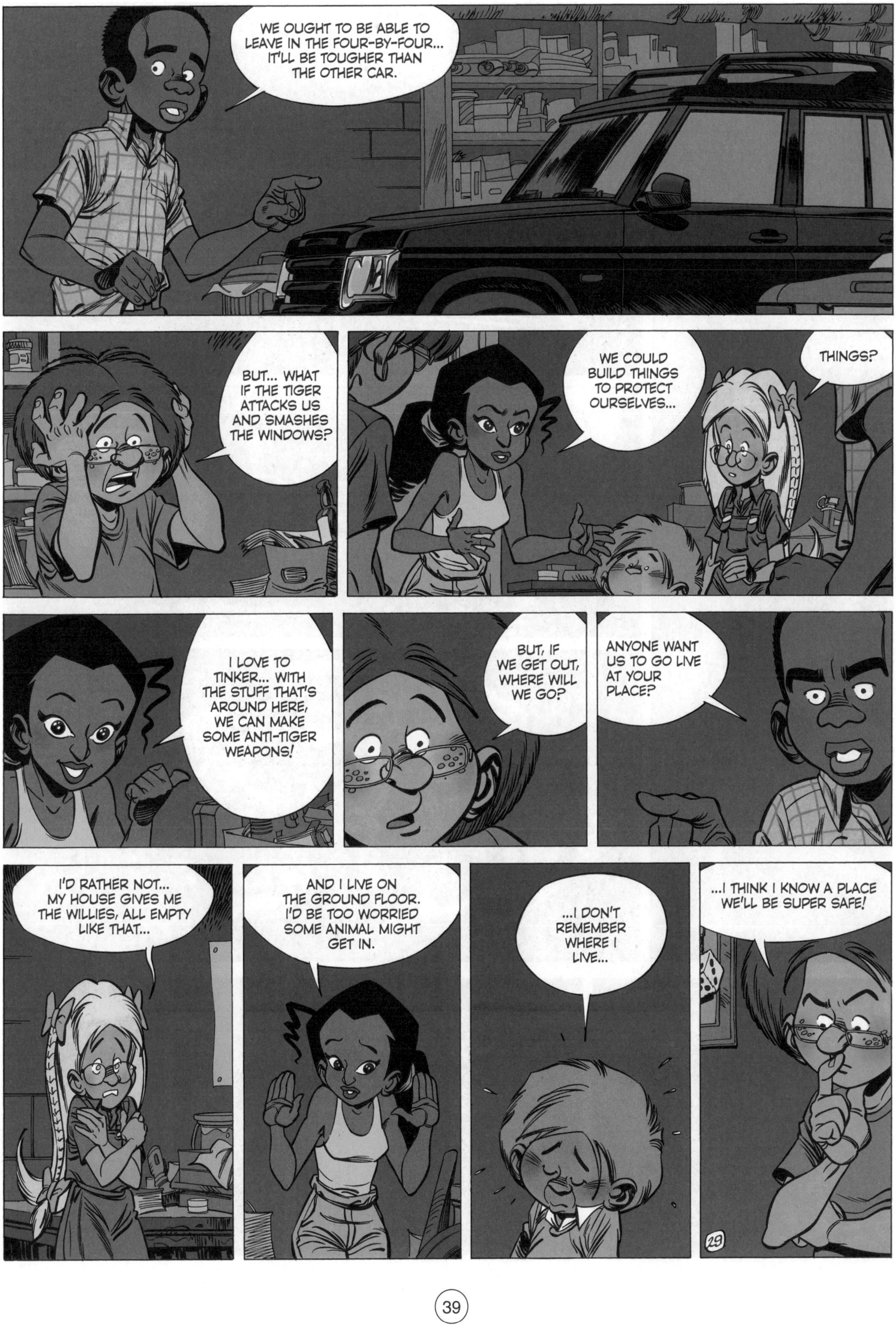
WE OUGHT TO BE ABLE TO LEAVE IN THE FOUR-BY-FOUR... IT'LL BE TOUGHER THAN THE OTHER CAR.
BUT... WHAT IF THE TIGER ATTACKS US AND SMASHES THE WINDOWS?
WE COULD BUILD THINGS TO PROTECT OURSELVES...
THINGS?
I LOVE TO TINKER... WITH THE STUFF THAT'S AROUND HERE, WE CAN MAKE SOME ANTI-TIGER WEAPONS!
BUT, IF WE GET OUT, WHERE WILL WE GO?
ANYONE WANT US TO GO LIVE AT YOUR PLACE?
I'D RATHER NOT... MY HOUSE GIVES ME THE WILLIES, ALL EMPTY LIKE THAT...
AND I LIVE ON THE GROUND FLOOR. I'D BE TOO WORRIED SOME ANIMAL MIGHT GET IN.
...I DON'T REMEMBER WHERE I LIVE...
...I THINK I KNOW A PLACE WE'LL BE SUPER SAFE!
29

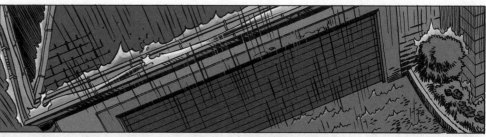

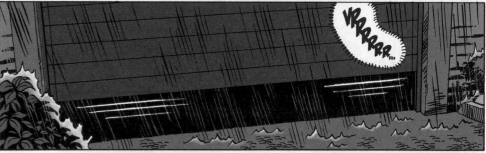

VRRRRR...

D'YOU THINK WE CAN GO?

WELL, WE CAN'T SPEND THE REST OF OUR LIVES IN THIS GARAGE, CAN WE?

BRR

KRRRRMM

I DON'T SEE THE TIGER!

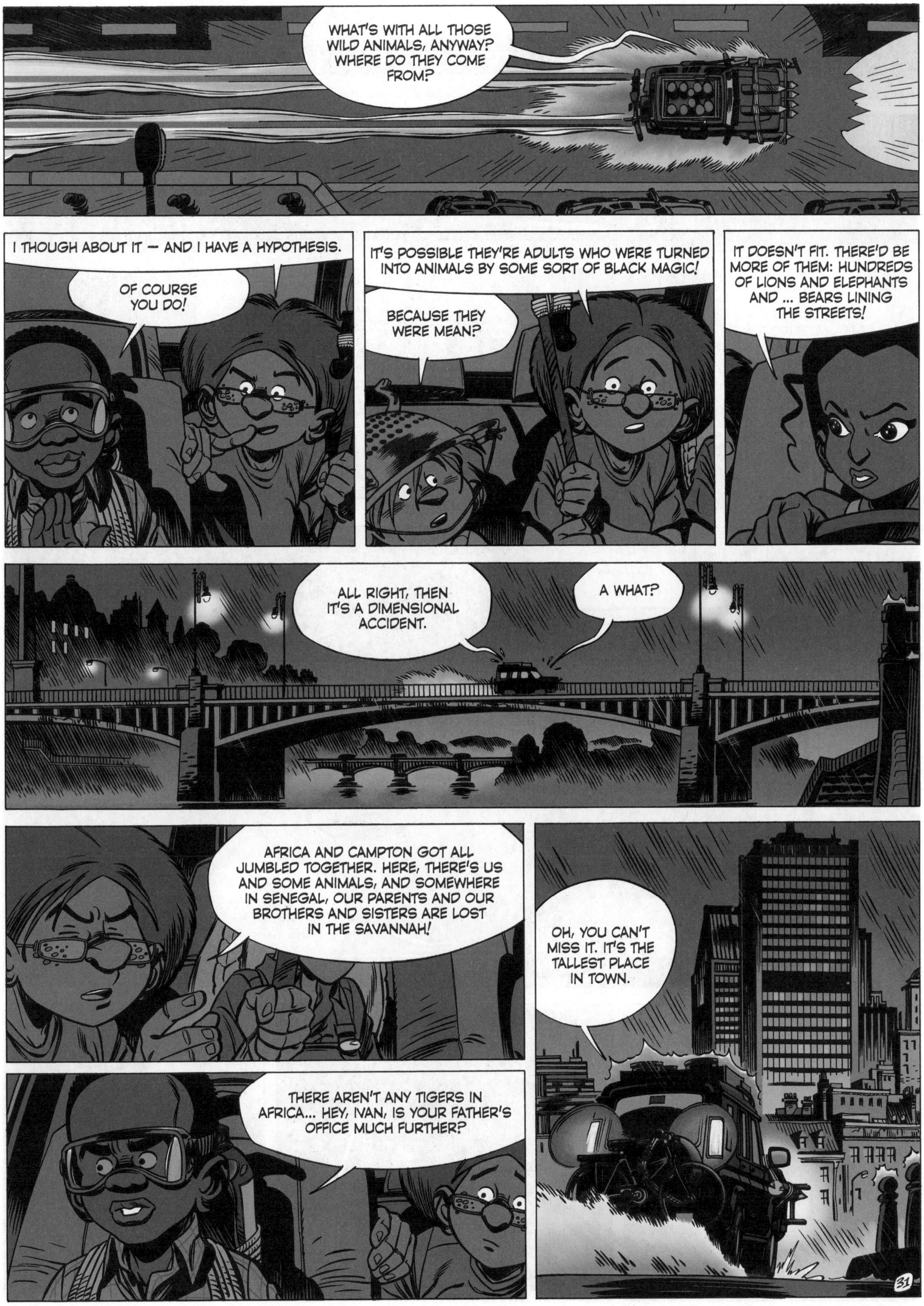
WHAT'S WITH ALL THOSE WILD ANIMALS, ANYWAY? WHERE DO THEY COME FROM?
I THOUGH ABOUT IT — AND I HAVE A HYPOTHESIS.
OF COURSE YOU DO!
IT'S POSSIBLE THEY'RE ADULTS WHO WERE TURNED INTO ANIMALS BY SOME SORT OF BLACK MAGIC!
BECAUSE THEY WERE MEAN?
IT DOESN'T FIT. THERE'D BE MORE OF THEM: HUNDREDS OF LIONS AND ELEPHANTS AND ... BEARS LINING THE STREETS!
ALL RIGHT, THEN IT'S A DIMENSIONAL ACCIDENT.
A WHAT?
AFRICA AND CAMPTON GOT ALL JUMBLED TOGETHER. HERE, THERE'S US AND SOME ANIMALS, AND SOMEWHERE IN SENEGAL, OUR PARENTS AND OUR BROTHERS AND SISTERS ARE LOST IN THE SAVANNAH!
THERE AREN'T ANY TIGERS IN AFRICA... HEY, IVAN, IS YOUR FATHER'S OFFICE MUCH FURTHER?
OH, YOU CAN'T MISS IT. IT'S THE TALLEST PLACE IN TOWN.
31

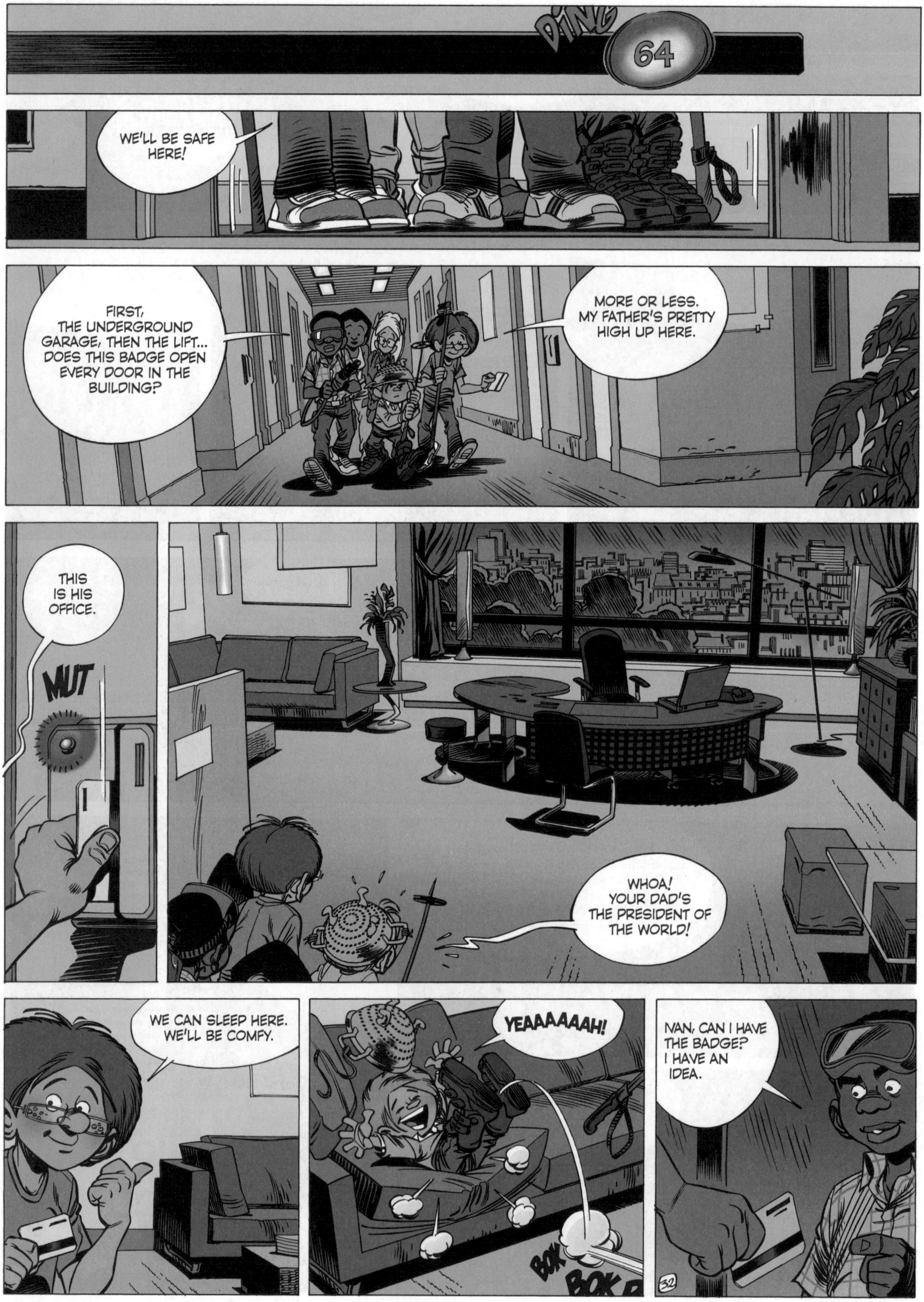
DING
64
WE'LL BE SAFE HERE!
FIRST, THE UNDERGROUND GARAGE, THEN THE LIFT... DOES THIS BADGE OPEN EVERY DOOR IN THE BUILDING?
MORE OR LESS. MY FATHER'S PRETTY HIGH UP HERE.
THIS IS HIS OFFICE.
MUT
WHOA! YOUR DAD'S THE PRESIDENT OF THE WORLD!
WE CAN SLEEP HERE. WE'LL BE COMFY.
YEAAAAAAH!
BOK
BOK
IVAN, CAN I HAVE THE BADGE? I HAVE AN IDEA.

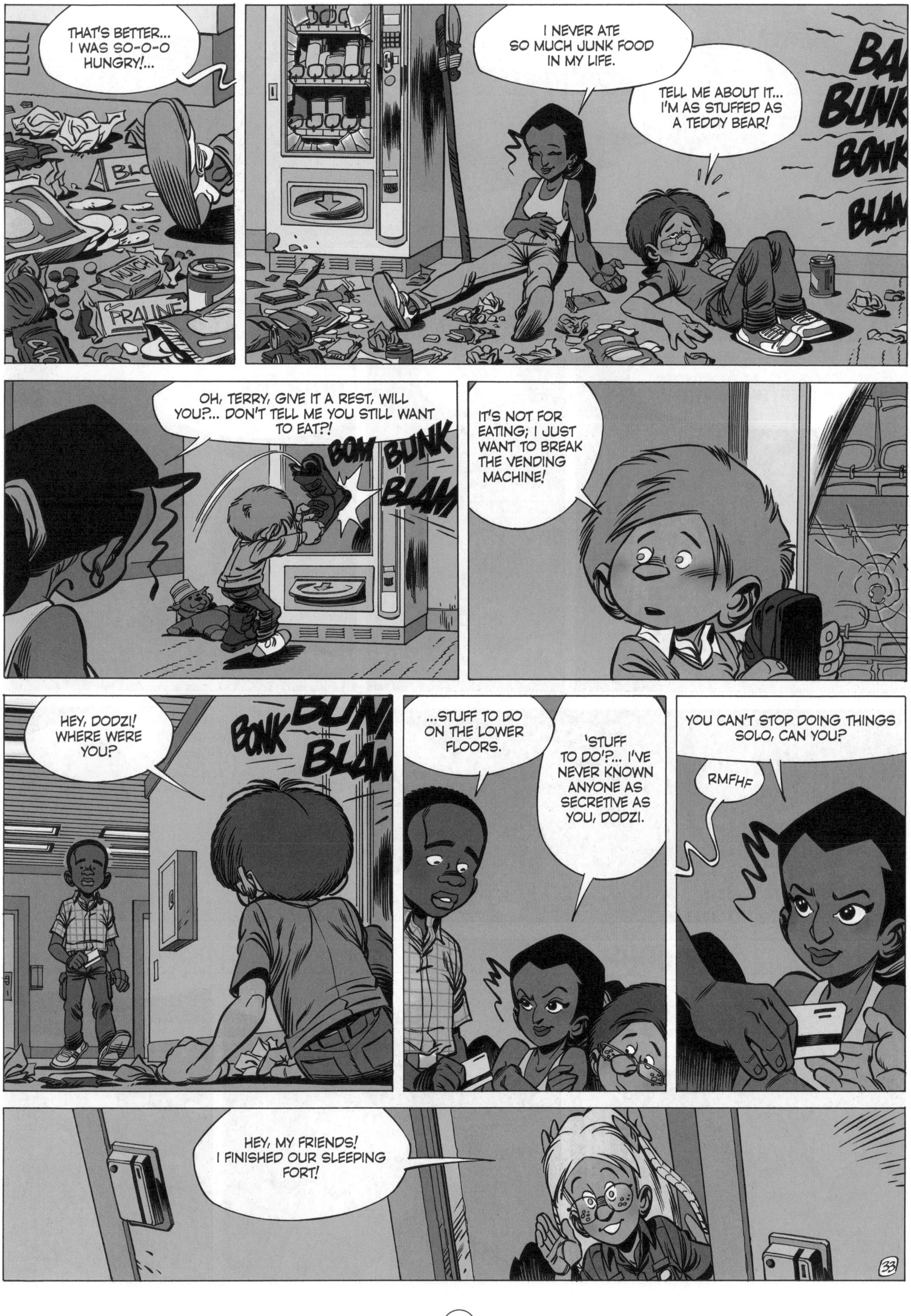

THAT'S BETTER... I WAS SO-O-O HUNGRY!...
I NEVER ATE SO MUCH JUNK FOOD IN MY LIFE.
TELL ME ABOUT IT... I'M AS STUFFED AS A TEDDY BEAR!
BUNK
BONK
OH, TERRY, GIVE IT A REST, WILL YOU?... DON'T TELL ME YOU STILL WANT TO EAT?!
BOM
BUNK
BLAM
IT'S NOT FOR EATING; I JUST WANT TO BREAK THE VENDING MACHINE!
HEY, DODZI! WHERE WERE YOU?
BONK
...STUFF TO DO ON THE LOWER FLOORS.
'STUFF TO DO'?... I'VE NEVER KNOWN ANYONE AS SECRETIVE AS YOU, DODZI.
YOU CAN'T STOP DOING THINGS SOLO, CAN YOU?
RMFHF
HEY, MY FRIENDS! I FINISHED OUR SLEEPING FORT!
33

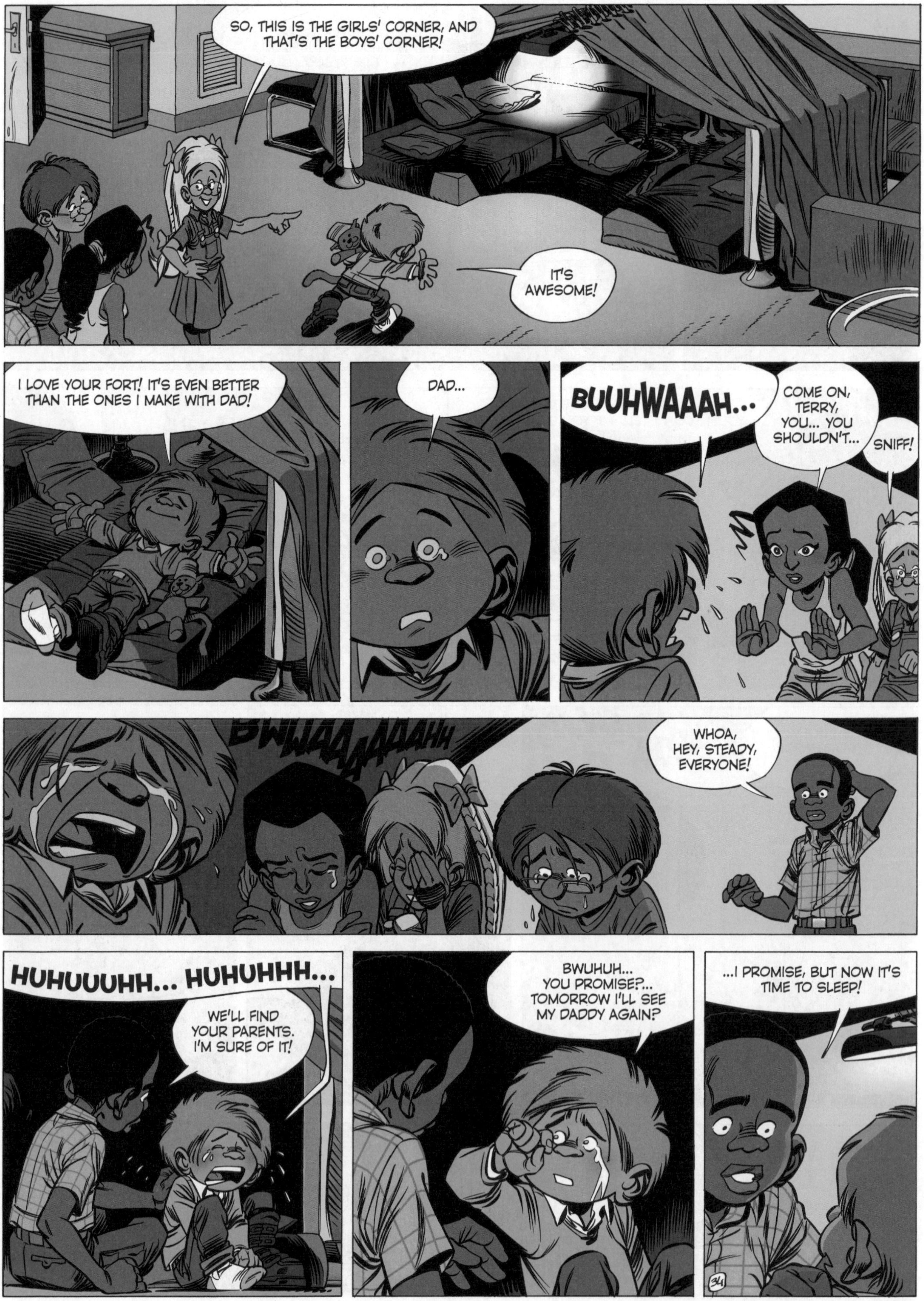
SO, THIS IS THE GIRLS' CORNER, AND THAT'S THE BOYS' CORNER!
IT'S AWESOME!
I LOVE YOUR FORT! IT'S EVEN BETTER THAN THE ONES I MAKE WITH DAD!
DAD...
BUUHWAAAH...
COME ON, TERRY, YOU... YOU SHOULDN'T...
SNIFF!
BWAAAAAAAHH
WHOA, HEY, STEADY, EVERYONE!
HUHUUUHH... HUHUHHH...
WE'LL FIND YOUR PARENTS. I'M SURE OF IT!
BWUHUH... YOU PROMISE?... TOMORROW I'LL SEE MY DADDY AGAIN?
...I PROMISE, BUT NOW IT'S TIME TO SLEEP!

IT'S A GOOD THING WE HAVE YOU WITH US, DODZI... I THINK YOU'RE VERY BRAVE.

IT'S DIFFERENT FOR ME. I'M USED TO GETTING BY ON MY OWN... MY PARENTS DIED A LONG TIME AGO.

OH!

I'LL SAY A PRAYER FOR THEM, DODZI.

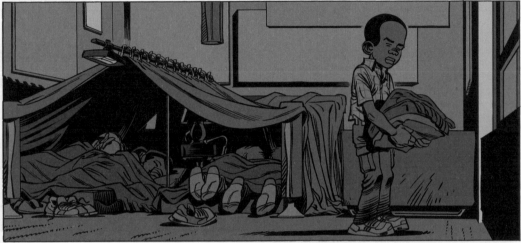

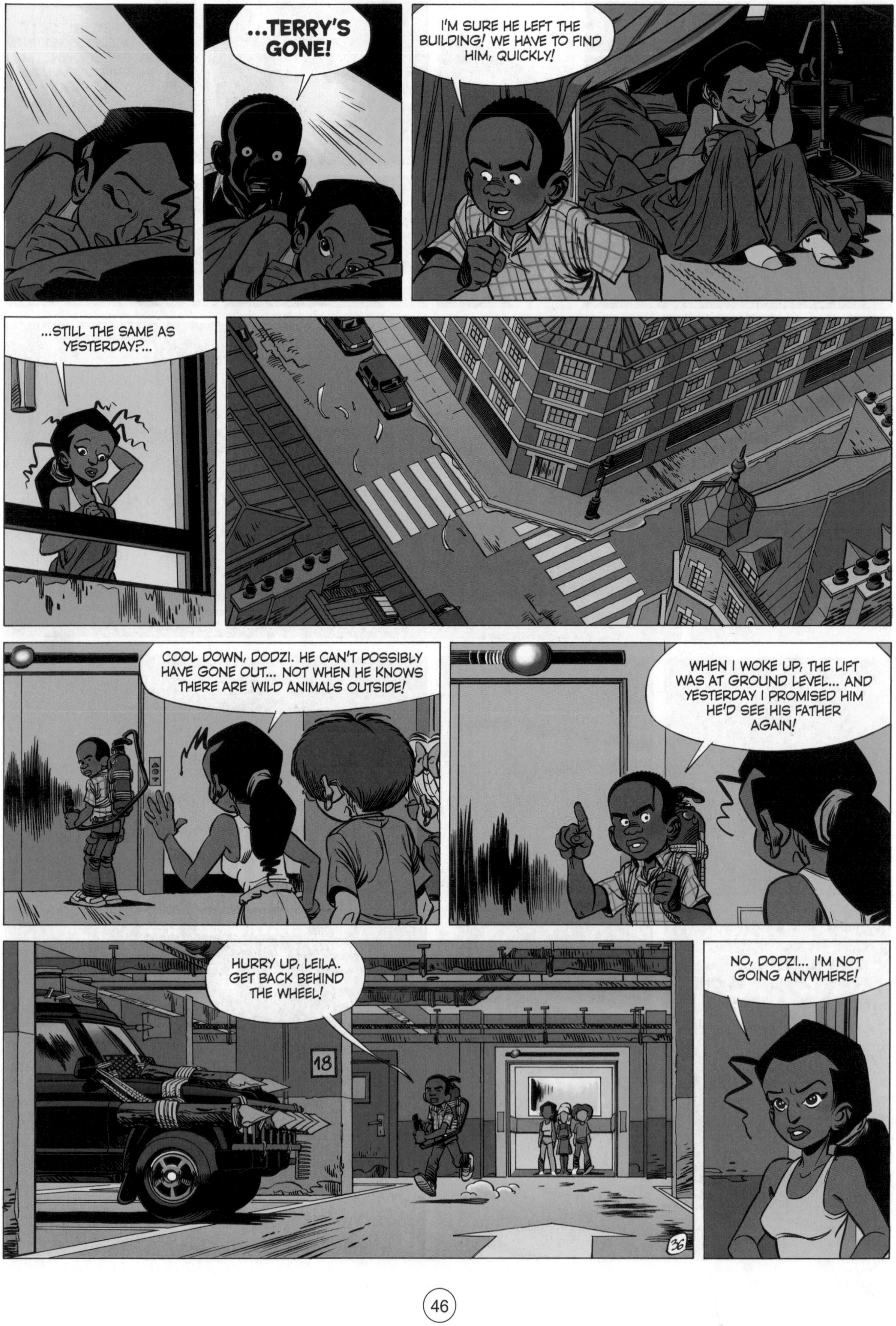
...TERRY'S GONE!
I'M SURE HE LEFT THE BUILDING! WE HAVE TO FIND HIM, QUICKLY!
...STILL THE SAME AS YESTERDAY?...
COOL DOWN, DODZI. HE CAN'T POSSIBLY HAVE GONE OUT... NOT WHEN HE KNOWS THERE ARE WILD ANIMALS OUTSIDE!
WHEN I WOKE UP, THE LIFT WAS AT GROUND LEVEL... AND YESTERDAY I PROMISED HIM HE'D SEE HIS FATHER AGAIN!
HURRY UP, LEILA. GET BACK BEHIND THE WHEEL!
18
36
NO, DODZI... I'M NOT GOING ANYWHERE!

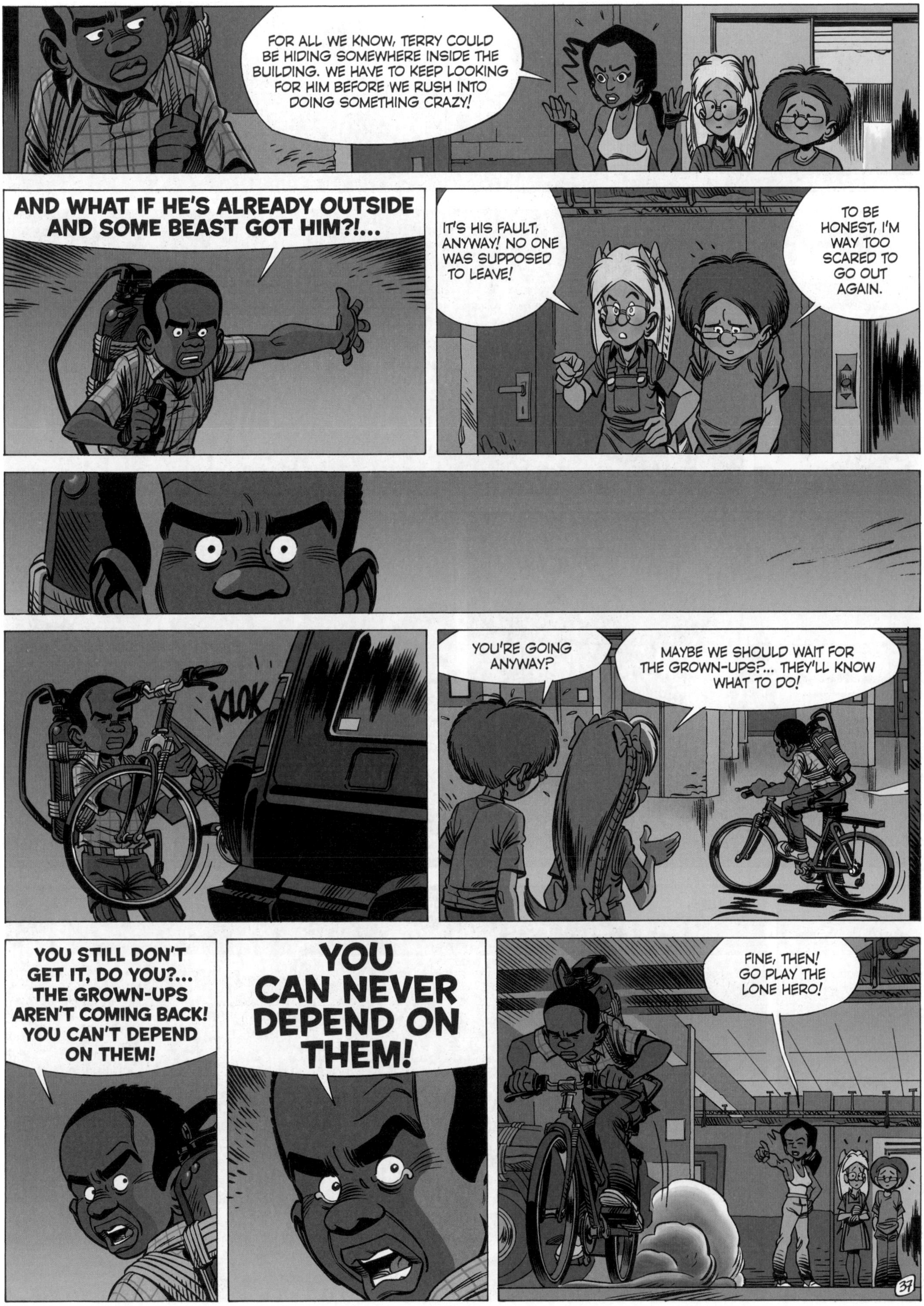
FOR ALL WE KNOW, TERRY COULD BE HIDING SOMEWHERE INSIDE THE BUILDING. WE HAVE TO KEEP LOOKING FOR HIM BEFORE WE RUSH INTO DOING SOMETHING CRAZY!
AND WHAT IF HE'S ALREADY OUTSIDE AND SOME BEAST GOT HIM?!...
IT'S HIS FAULT, ANYWAY! NO ONE WAS SUPPOSED TO LEAVE!
TO BE HONEST, I'M WAY TOO SCARED TO GO OUT AGAIN.
KLOK
YOU'RE GOING ANYWAY?
MAYBE WE SHOULD WAIT FOR THE GROWN-UPS?... THEY'LL KNOW WHAT TO DO!
YOU STILL DON'T GET IT, DO YOU?... THE GROWN-UPS AREN'T COMING BACK! YOU CAN'T DEPEND ON THEM!
YOU CAN NEVER DEPEND ON THEM!
FINE, THEN! GO PLAY THE LONE HERO!
37

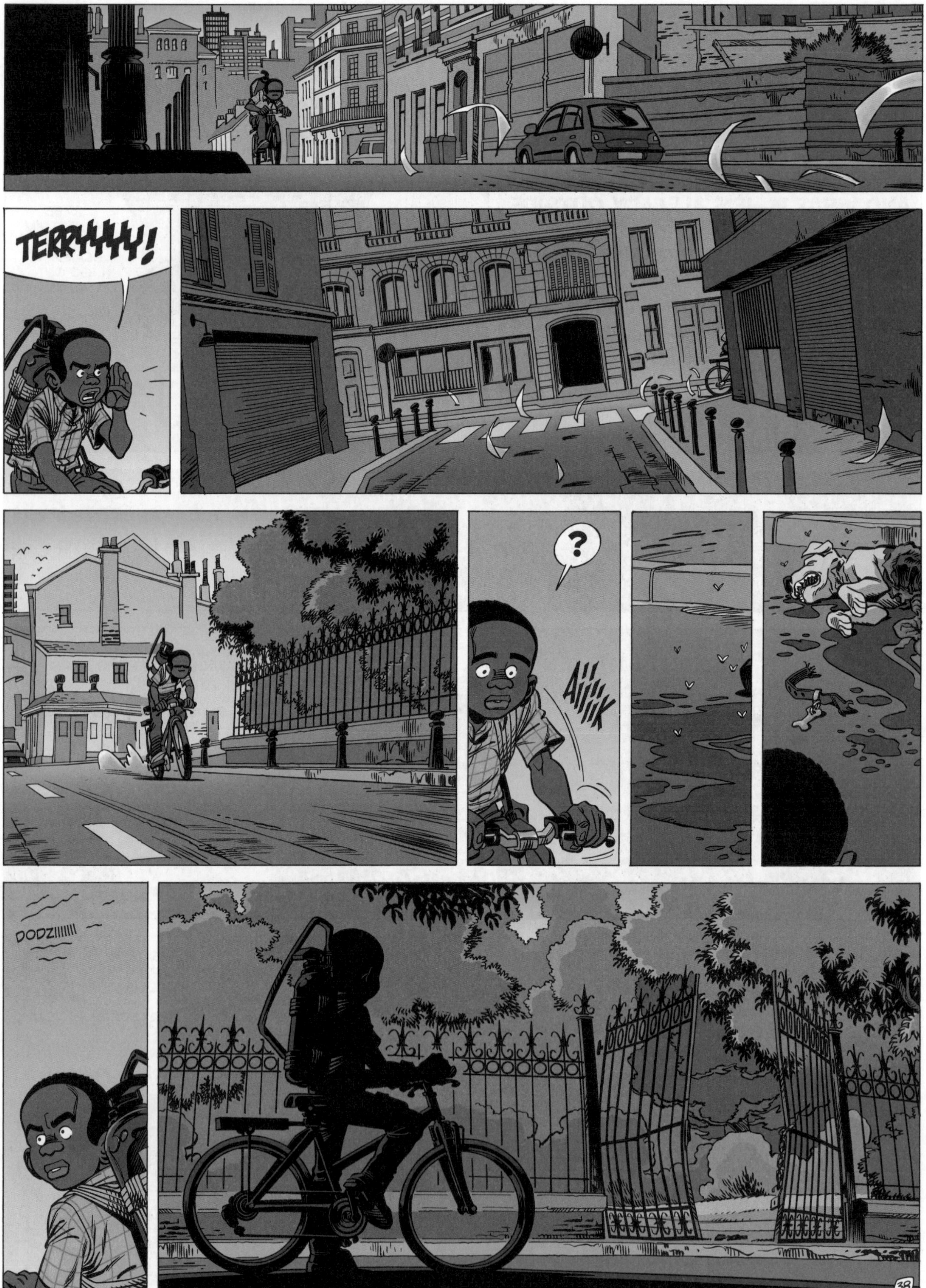
TERRYYYY!
?
AIIIIK
DODZIIIIII
38

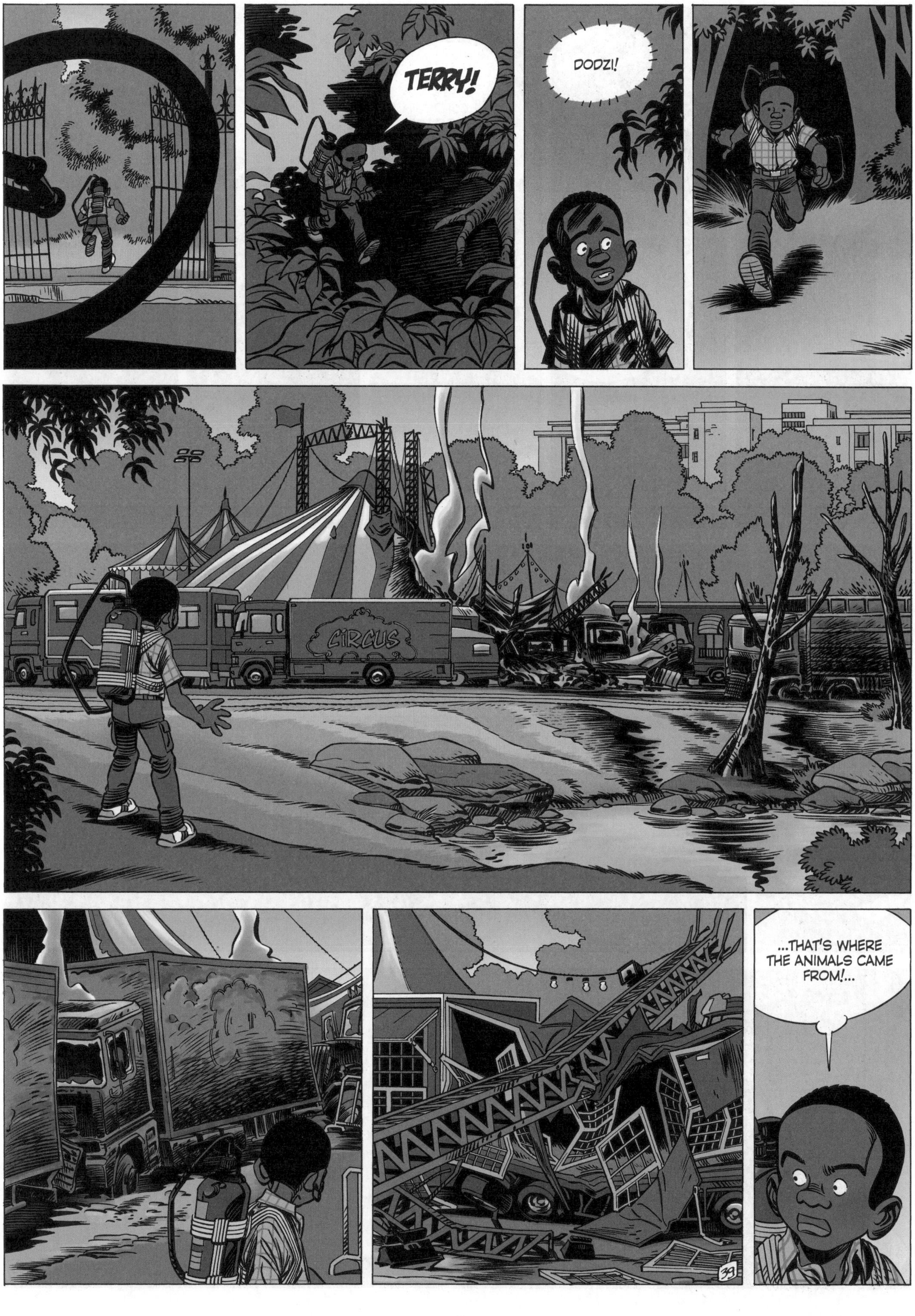

TERRY!
DODZI!
CIRCUS
...THAT'S WHERE THE ANIMALS CAME FROM!...

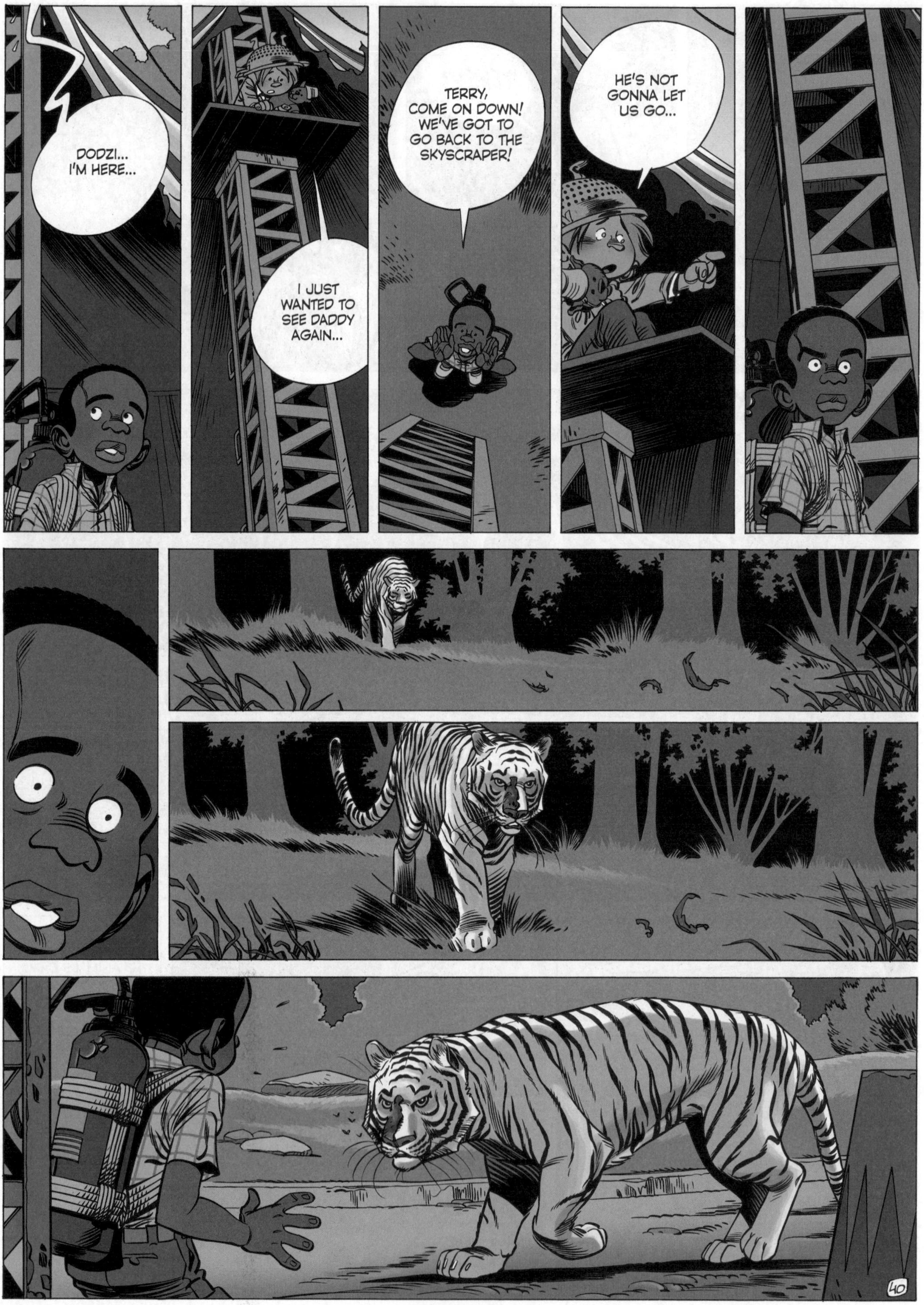
DODZI... I'M HERE...
I JUST WANTED TO SEE DADDY AGAIN...
TERRY, COME ON DOWN! WE'VE GOT TO GO BACK TO THE SKYSCRAPER!
HE'S NOT GONNA LET US GO...
40

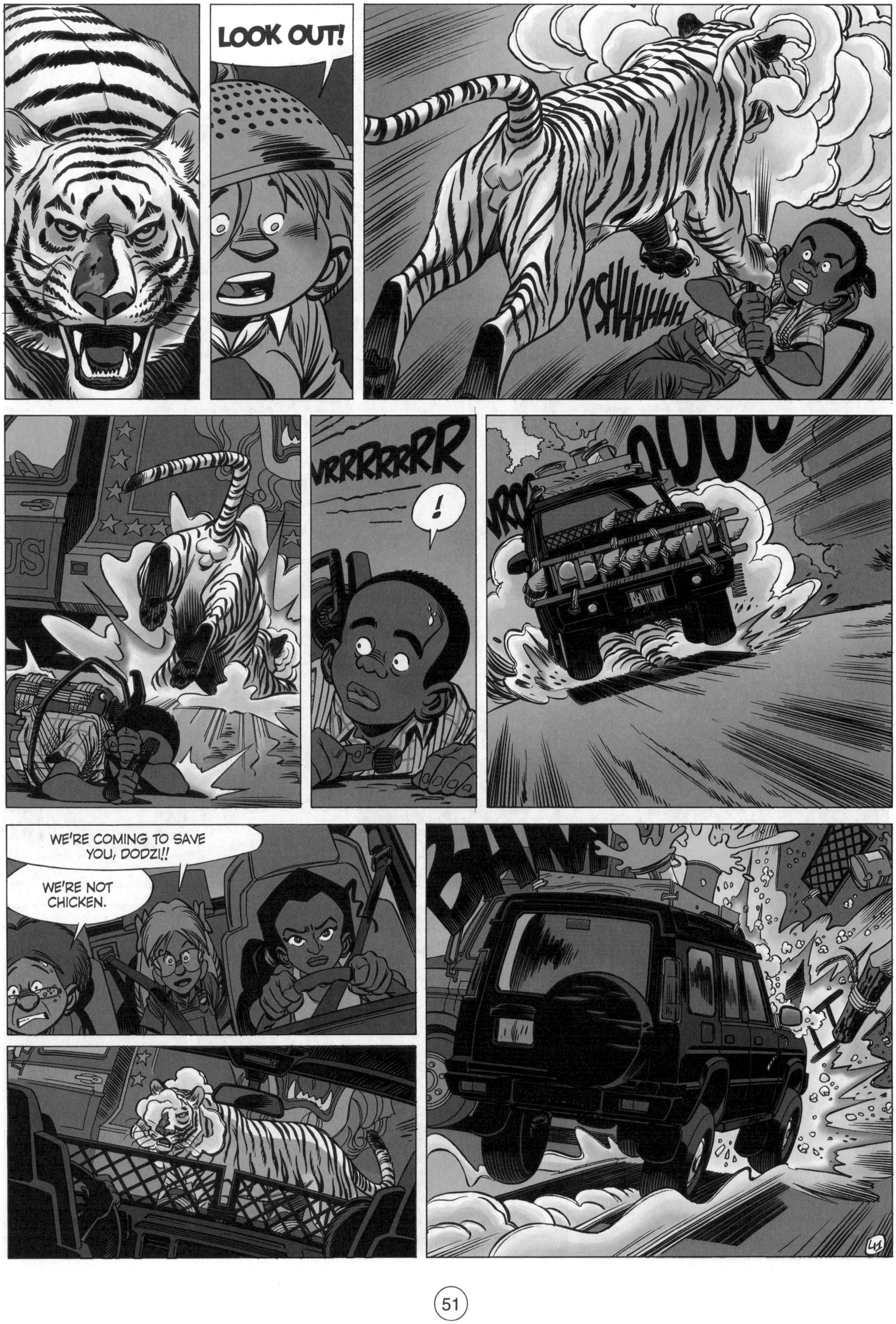

LOOK OUT!
PSHHHHHH
VRRRRRRR
!
WE'RE COMING TO SAVE YOU, DODZI!!
WE'RE NOT CHICKEN.

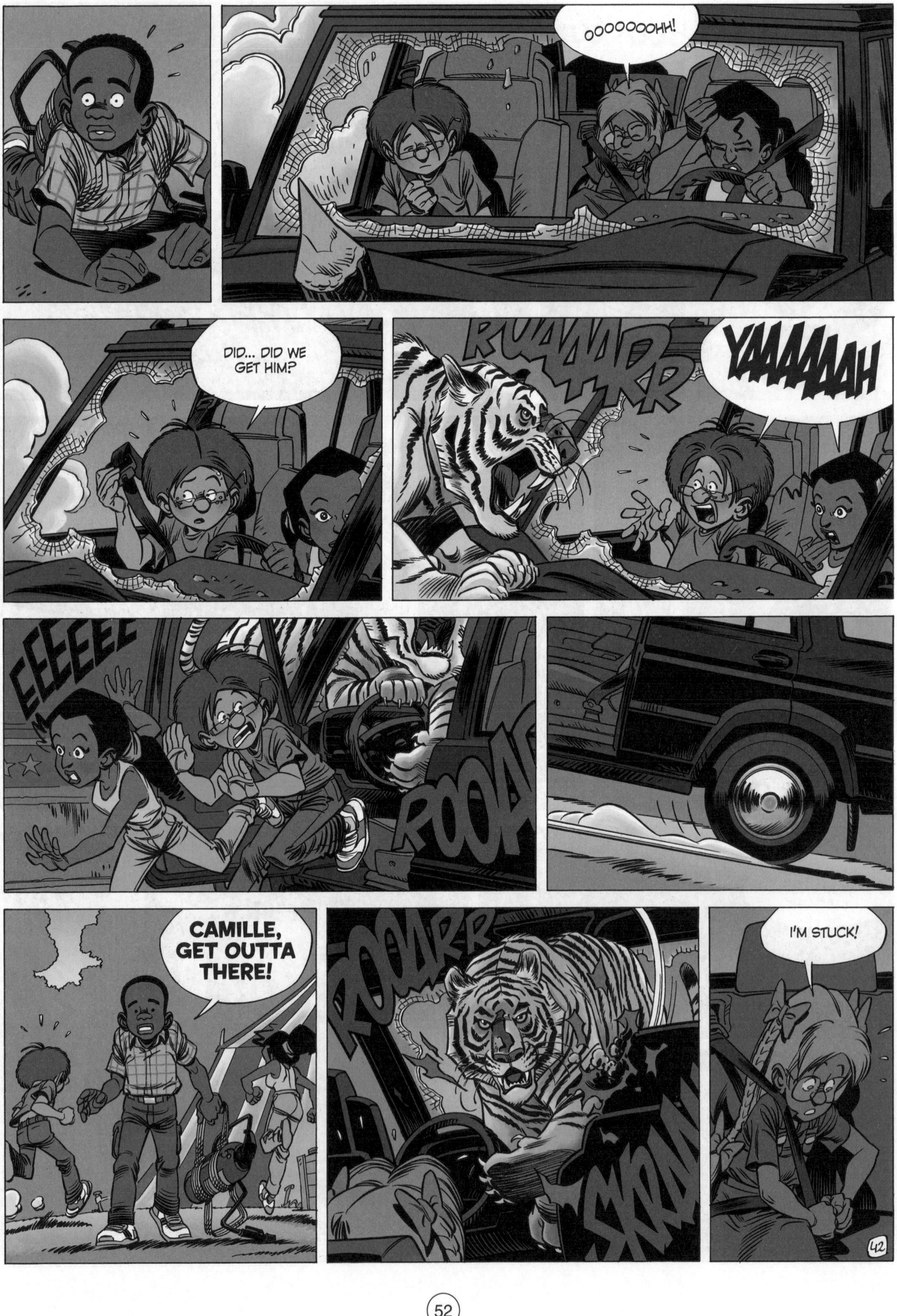

OOOOOOOHH!
DID... DID WE GET HIM?
RUAAARRR
YAAAAAAH
EEEEEE
ROOAA
CAMILLE, GET OUTTA THERE!
ROOARR
SCRAA
I'M STUCK!
42

RRROUARR
EEEEEEE!
DODZI! CAMILLE!
NO!
SPLASH!

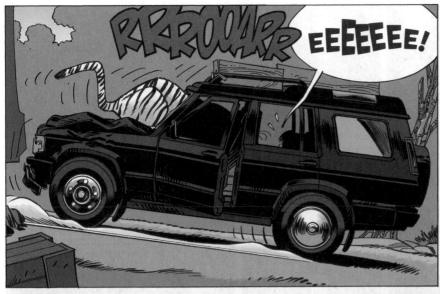

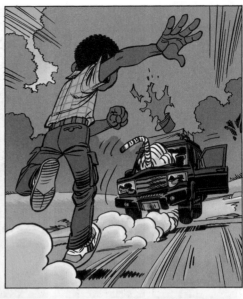

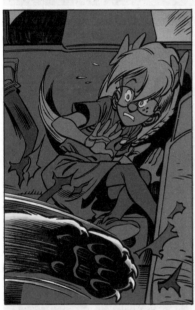

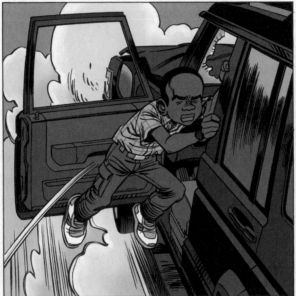

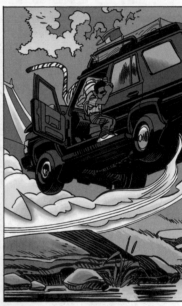

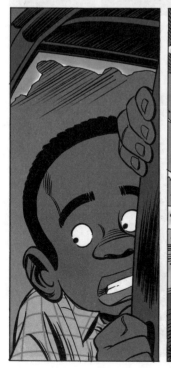

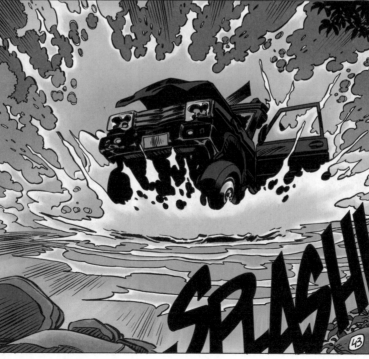

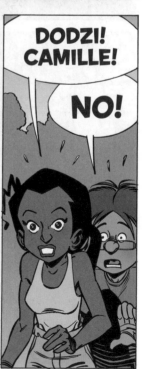

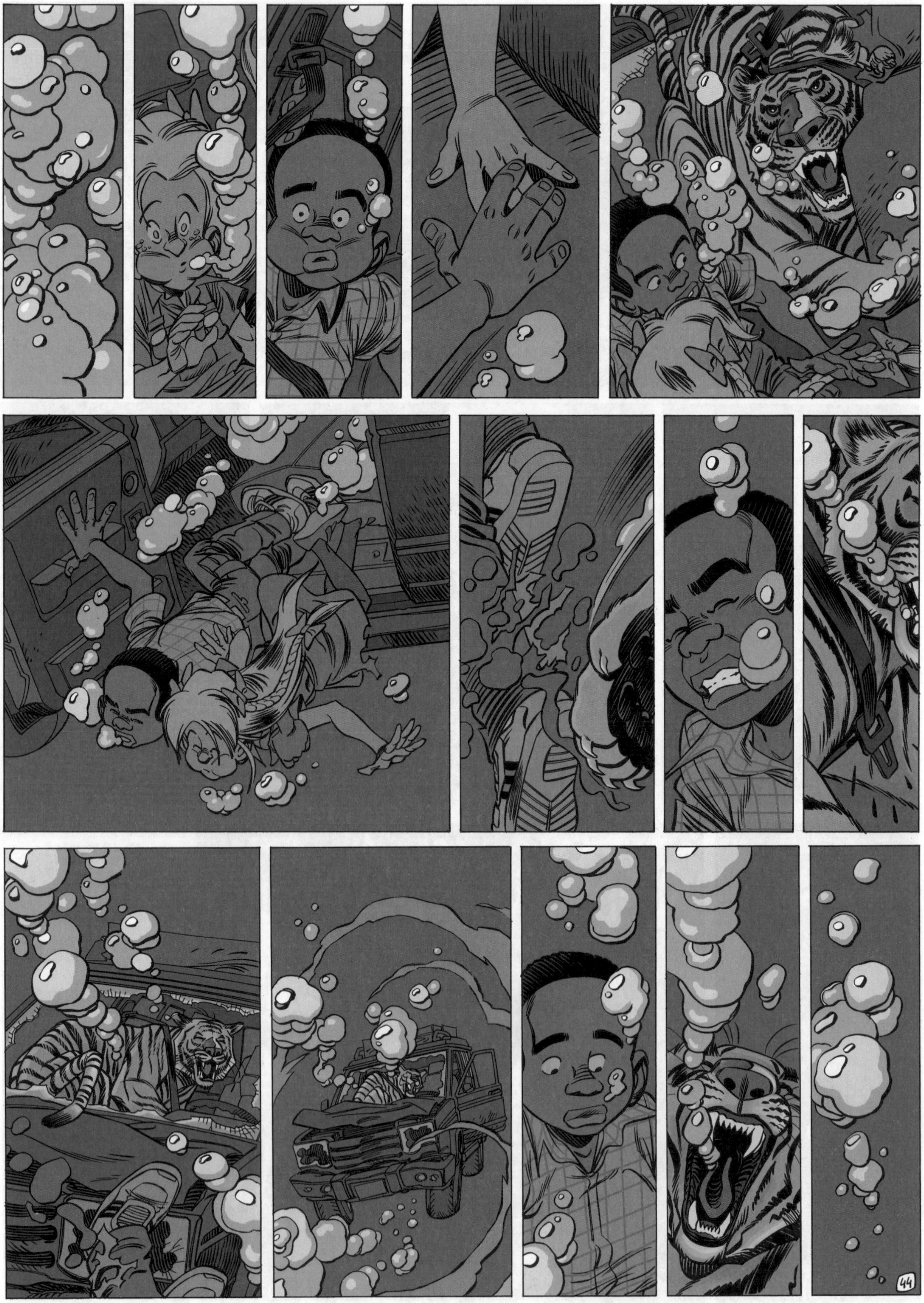
44

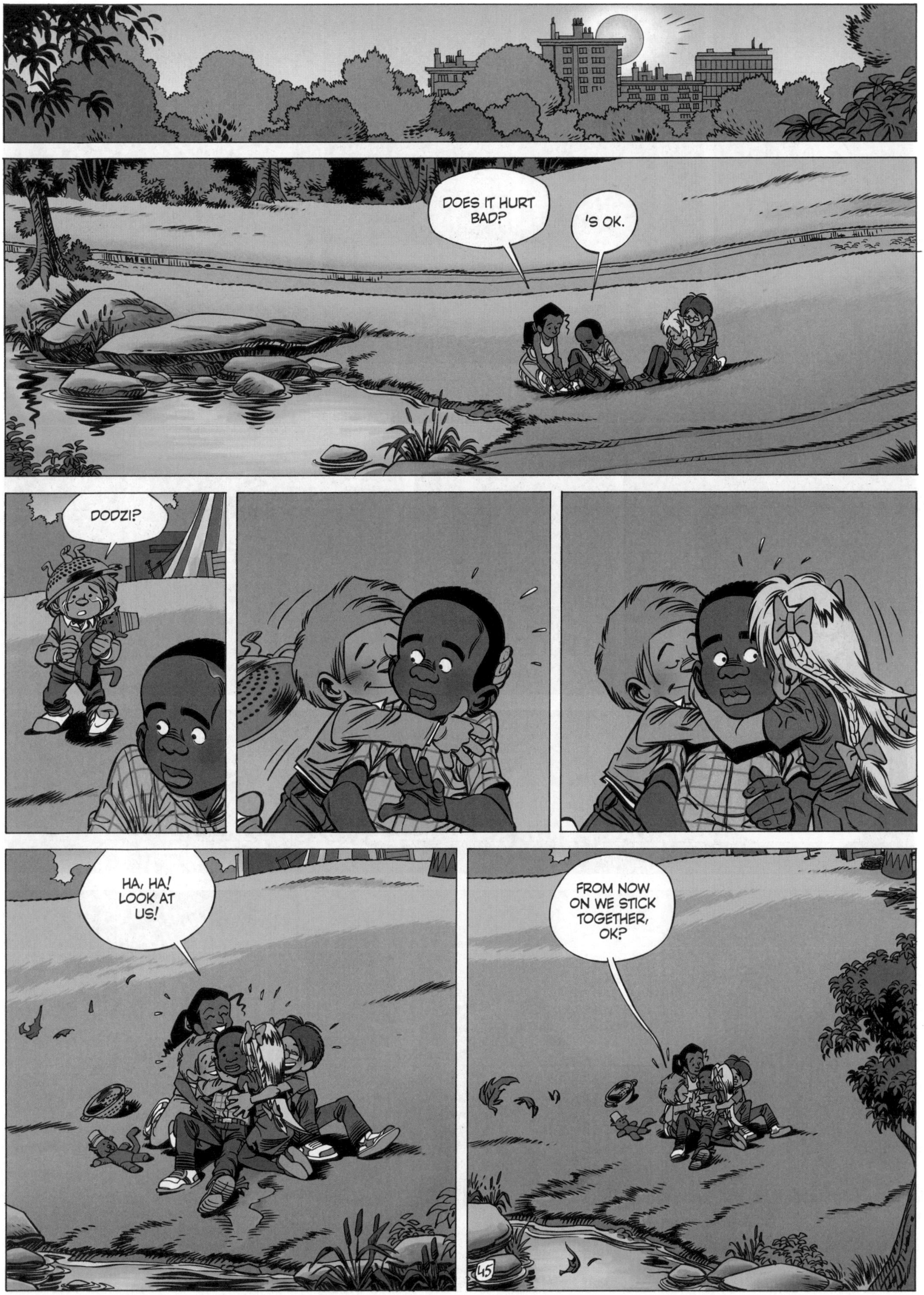
DOES IT HURT BAD?
'S OK.
DODZI?
HA, HA! LOOK AT US!
FROM NOW ON WE STICK TOGETHER, OK?
45

SHALL WE GO HOME?

YOU WERE RIGHT EARLIER WHEN YOU SAID WE COULDN'T COUNT ON THE GROWN-UPS ANY MORE.

I GOT A BIT CARRIED AWAY... THEY MAY STILL COME BACK, YOU KNOW.

IT'S POSSIBLE... BUT, IT'S ALSO POSSIBLE WE WON'T SEE THEM AGAIN IN A LONG TIME. WE STILL DON'T KNOW HOW THEY VANISHED...

...AND IN THE MEANTIME, WE'LL HAVE TO LEARN HOW TO GET BY WITHOUT THEM.

NOT A PROBLEM... WE'LL GET OURSELVES ORGANISED!

COULOURS: CERISE

VEHLMANN GAZZOTTI 2005

56